COMPASS

CREATING EXCEPTIONAL ORGANIZATIONS: A LEADER'S GUIDE

William F. Brandt, Jr.

WV WINTER VALE PRESS
Winchester, Virginia

COMPASS
Creating Exceptional Organizations: A Leader's Guide

by William F. Brandt, Jr.

Published by: Winter Vale Press
                  145 Creekside Lane
                  Winchester, VA 22606
Telephone: 540-999-6303
Fax: 540-665-8324
Website: www.WinterValePress.com
E-mail: ContactUs@WinterValePress.com

ISBN: 978-0-9883205-0-5
Library of Congress Control Number: 2012955360

First Edition. Printed in the United States of America
10 9 8 7 6 5 4 3 2 1

Cartoon on page 197 used with permission from The Cartoon Bank.
Page Design by One-On-One Book Production, West Hills, California

TO ELAINE

CONTENTS

SECTION 3
LESSONS

Contents

EXHIBITS

1

INTRODUCTION

American industry, by which I mean those for-profit and non-profit organizations that provide the bulk of our society's goods and services, has served us well, advancing the lives of people for over 200 years and helping to build a great nation. The foundation of this advancement is *capitalism*, which has as its premise, "the pursuit of self-interest benefits not only the individual but also society."

While this underlying premise has proved successful, it does have its limitations—and these limitations are increasing as our world becomes more complex, more interconnected and more interdependent. These conditions were exceedingly evident in the most recent financial crisis, where a few institutions—who absorbed substantial risks in the zealous pursuit of their own self-interests—hurt not only their own stakeholders but also had the potential to disrupt the world financial markets with disastrous consequences for all.

While this book acknowledges that the pursuit of self-interest has benefited society, it offers a new, more powerful paradigm—namely, the simultaneous pursuit of both "self-interest" and "concern for others." This new orientation provides a guide for behavior that reflects both the greatest aspirations of humankind and the reality of the world in which we live. This paradigm is not in opposition to the industry structure that has fostered our historic success, but rather stands upon the shoulders of what has come before.

We can act according to this new paradigm by creating what I call *exceptional organizations*—which are:

- *viable*—in that they achieve their purposes and do so while acting according to society's highest values

- *sustainable*—by remaining viable over time

- *valued*—in that all stakeholders—owners, employees, clients, providers and communities—see their association with these enterprises as being worthy, whereby they benefit to a significantly greater degree than they would with competing entities.

Such organizations foster the personal, professional and moral growth of their members and are, by definition, valued by society because society is one of their stakeholders.

An exceptional organization is potentially more powerful than a traditional organization because all of its members—by pursuing both their own self-interests and concerns for others—have a shared interest in sustaining the viability and value-creation of the enterprise. This is in sharp contrast to members of a traditional organization, who, by acting in their own self-interests, relate to the entity strictly on a transactional basis. Such members attempt to receive "the highest value for services rendered," without regard for the enterprise as a whole or its other stakeholders.

Exceptional organizations are also more powerful because their leaders focus upon long-term viability and value-creation rather than attempting to optimize their own or any other stakeholder's interests. By doing so, these enterprises are more likely to prosper and grow to the greater benefit of all. Paradoxically, this means, for example, that shareholders will likely receive higher long-term financial returns when their organizations do *not* attempt to "maximize shareholder value" than when they do.

PURPOSE

This is a "how to" book. It is intended for those leaders who in their hearts and minds are already committed to creating organizations consistent with the new paradigm but who have not yet found a vehicle for getting there.

By using this book as a compass, leaders will likely:

- expand their horizons of what is possible

- increase the likelihood of creating the type of organizations they truly desire

- reduce the time necessary to accomplish this task

- reduce, but not eliminate, the costs and consequences of missteps and false starts along the way.

AUDIENCES

There are many types of organizations. Our focus here is on for-profit and non-profit entities that vary by size, scope and complexity. Such enterprises include large corporations, small businesses, universities, hospitals, non-governmental organizations and charitable institutions. While each has its differences, they all have two traits in common. First, to remain sustainable they must generate a positive cash flow over time, where incoming cash exceeds outgoing disbursements. Second, the principles and techniques used to create exceptional organizations are applicable to them all.

The primary audience for this book are leaders and members of enterprises who aspire to enhance organizational effectiveness either by engaging in a comprehensive transformation of their institutions' entire behaviors or by adopting appropriate principles and methodologies to achieve specific tasks. The concepts and tools presented are likely applicable to teams and departments within a larger entity even though that entity might not pursue an overall initiative.

The secondary audience is comprised of those who desire to learn about exceptional enterprises and to assist in their creation. Included in this category are advisors, consultants, coaches, teachers and students, among others.

WHAT ARE THE KEY ELEMENTS OF EXCEPTIONAL ORGANIZATIONS?

Relatively few organizations are exceptional. Those that are can be characterized not only by the results they achieve—being viable, sustainable and valued—but also by the *key elements* that comprise them.

The answers to four questions are the basis of these elements:

QUESTION	ANSWER
Why do we do it?	Purpose
What do we do?	Action
How do we do it?	Culture
Who does it?	People

We can define these elements as follows:

- **Purpose**—why we exist, the mission the organization pursues

- **Action**—the work we do to achieve our purpose

- **Culture**—the values, beliefs, traditions and processes that guide behavior

- **People**—the organization's members who do this work.

Each element has an *organizing principle* or theme that focuses behavior toward the achievement of the organization's mission.

ELEMENT	ORGANIZING PRINCIPLE
Purpose	Inspiration
Action	Vision-Driven
Culture	Value-Based
People	Right-Person / Right Job

PURPOSE: The organizing principle for "purpose" is *inspiration*. The enterprise inspires its members to act for a cause greater than their own self-interests. Such inspiration gives individuals a sense of meaning in alignment with the organization's purpose.

In the absence of this principle, the organization must assume that its members will act soley in their own self-interests. If this is the case, the organization is forced to utilize rewards and punishments as its primary source of motivation. This places a great burden on the organization to structure its reward-and-punishment systems to be in complete harmony with its purpose and with all of the expected actions required to achieve it. Furthermore, the absence of this principle reduces the level of commitment by members and inhibits their experiencing a sense of worth and well-being that comes from serving a greater cause.

ACTION: A *vision-driven* organization takes action to achieve an end result that, when achieved, supports the entity's purpose. All activity is focused upon the achievement of the vision, and all decisions are made based upon the merits of whether or not a particular action supports it.

A component of this organizing principle is a *business strategy,* or business model, which creates a competitive advantage. When achieved, this advantage will generate a significant and sustainable cash flow. Work is aligned to execute the strategy which in turn supports the overall vision. The organization gathers both external and internal feedback to adjust its actions as necessary.

Without a vision-driven organizing principle, actions are frequently independent of the organization's purpose. This is especially true when the motivation for action shifts to meeting the needs of individuals higher up in hierarchy. When this occurs, decisions are made not on their merits but rather to please the boss, which leads to wasted or misguided efforts.

CULTURE: The culture describes *how* members behave as they work. It consists of the organization's values, beliefs, traditions and processes. A *value-based* culture of an exceptional organization behaves according to its expected norms which are consistent with the highest values of society.

Not being a value-based culture will result in the organization's members acting according to whatever they think is appropriate for the entity and themselves. This will result in behaviors often at variance with the organization's purpose, mission and values.

PEOPLE: The organizing principle that marshals the organization's people is the employment of the *right person in the right job*. All human resource activities focus upon structuring each position to be held by a highly-qualified and committed individual.

Not having the right person in the right job inhibits the organization's ability to accomplish its vision. Furthermore, placing people in jobs where they are unable to perform creates a hardship for them personally, either because of the stress of not doing well or the prospect of losing their positions.

Exhibit 1.1 shows the interrelationship of the four organizing principles relative to the key elements of exceptional organizations. The four elements interrelate with each other to form the organization as a whole with each element reinforcing the other.

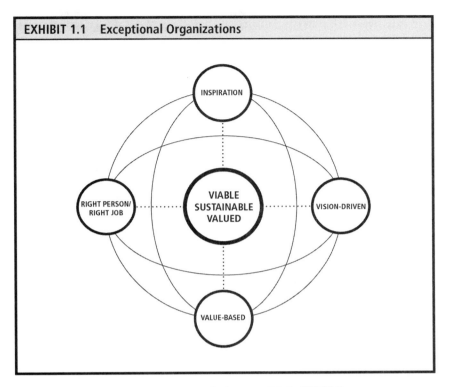

EXHIBIT 1.1   Exceptional Organizations

INSPIRATION

RIGHT PERSON/
RIGHT JOB

VIABLE
SUSTAINABLE
VALUED

VISION-DRIVEN

VALUE-BASED

HOW THIS BOOK WILL HELP

This book provides a number of beliefs, tools and techniques that support the key elements described above. These principles can be applied individually to address tasks or collectively as part of a broad-based organizational-change initiative. When applied correctly, such an initiative will result in the organization and its members having:

- a shared vision of the organization's aspirations
- a shared understanding of current reality
- common beliefs and values
- highly effective and universally applicable tools and processes
- a common language across the enterprise.

As these attributes are embraced, the organization will slowly reach a critical mass after which it will quickly move toward becoming exceptional.

FORMAT

Chapter 2 describes how to use this book. From Chapter 3 forward, the book is divided into five sections. The first presents a case study of American Woodmark's attempt to become exceptional. I cofounded and served as CEO of American Woodmark, which is the third largest manufacturer of kitchen cabinets nationally. The case study provides an understanding of the challenges facing those who attempt a similar path and gives the reader a context for the ideas included in the essays and lessons that follow.

The second section is a collection of essays designed to challenge traditional beliefs about organizations and offers readers some new perspectives. The essays are grouped into four categories. "The Vision" describes what is possible—the results desired—for both exceptional organizations and individuals within them. "The Leader" presents the leadership imperatives necessary to create and sustain exceptional institutions. "Processes and Tools" offer various beliefs, insights and techniques in support of the four key elements of exceptional organizations. Finally, "The Journey" shares the challenges that face those attempting to create such entities.

The third section is a series of lessons that provide education and training for specific tools and processes that when applied will form a framework for creating exceptional organizations. The lessons are divided into the same four categories as the essays: "The Vision," "The Leader," "Processes and Tools" and "The Journey."

The fourth section is an interview with John P. Howe, III, M.D., the CEO of Project HOPE, an international humanitarian aide organization. Project HOPE is using materials now included in this book to support its efforts to become exceptional.

The interview shows readers how a different type of organization is applying the book's principles and methodologies.

The fifth section presents a step-by-step guide for deciding whether an organization should undertake a broad-based initiative to become exceptional, and if it should, how best to proceed. It also references a unique feature of this book whereby readers who utilize items offered on the book's website will be able to customize the use of this material for specific presentations for particular audiences. Finally, this section shares my closing perspective.

THE JOURNEY

No book has all the answers for creating exceptional organizations. All such entities are viable, sustainable and valued. How they manifest these attributes, however, is unique to each. Furthermore, every organization starts at a different place. Therefore, getting from where you are to where you want to be must be a unique path that you develop together with your team and organization. At best, this book provides a compass to guide you toward your destination. While I hope this book will serve as a catalyst to help you think and behave differently, the onus is upon you to undertake your own journey and create the results that meet your aspirations. It is your choice. As challenging as such a journey may be, once completed, it will be well worth the effort. It will be transformational for both you and your organization.

2

HOW TO USE THIS BOOK

This book has two particular uses. The first is to address specific topics or concerns, and the second is to assist in the development of broad-based efforts to create exceptional organizations. The "Essays" and "Lessons" sections speak to its use in particular situations. Exhibit 2.1, included at the end of this chapter, is a subject index that shows where specific topics are addressed. All sections are relevant to the creation of organization-wide initiatives.

AMERICAN WOODMARK CASE STUDY

The case study provides a narrative of American Woodmark's efforts to become exceptional. It is of particular value to those leaders who are trying to understand what to expect in taking this path. While this case study provides a context for both the essays and lessons which follow, it is not necessary to read it prior to using these materials.

ESSAYS

The essays are intended to challenge your thinking and pique your curiosity. They can be used for individual reading or as topics for group discussion. They can also be read in anticipation of lesson presentations on related topics.

LESSONS

Each lesson applies to a particular situation. Since each is independent of the other, they can be used in any sequence desired. The lessons are educational in nature but where appropriate also focus upon skill-building. They are easy to learn but powerful in application. While each lesson stands on its own, collectively they act as building blocks that support the creation of exceptional organizations.

AN INTERVIEW

The interview with John Howe, III, M.D., President of Project HOPE will give the reader a perspective on one leader's attempt to create an exceptional enterprise. It will be of particular benefit to leaders and their senior leadership teams who are considering their own such ventures.

IMPLEMENTATION

Chapter 37 helps leaders to understand whether or not their organizations are ready to pursue a broad-based cultural-change effort and, if they are, how they should best proceed. Included in the chapter are hints and suggestions based upon the experiences of others.

Chapter 38 describes the book's website, which offers individualized articles based upon materials from this book. Included in the website are PowerPoint™ slides of each lesson for group presentation. These materials can be downloaded from the site. Where providing this book in its entirety may be neither necessary nor appropriate, leaders can create customized presentations for particular audiences. A useful way to present specific topics to groups is to provide relevant essays prior to a group session, to conduct a lesson on the topic utilizing the PowerPoint™ slides, and finally to give the written version of the lesson as a follow up.

EXHIBIT 2.1   Subject Index

TOPIC	CHAPTER	PAGE
Beliefs	24: Culture	150
Business Model	14: Yes, Even For Non-Profits 22: Vision-Driven	93 130
Business Strategy	14: Yes, Even For Non-Profits 22: Vision-Driven	93 130
Capitalism	1: Introduction 12: The Survival of the Fittest	1 85
Celebrity CEO's	7: The Servant as Leader	65
Charismatic Leadership	8: Imagine and Inspire	69
Competition	12: The Survival of the Fittest	85
Controlling Events	21: "Any Luck?"	121
Cooperation	12: The Survival of the Fittest	85
Creative Orientation	10: "What Do I Want?"	78
Culture and Cultural Change	17: Guidance from Gandhi 24: Culture 34: Cultural Change	107 150 254
Discourse: Dialogue, Discussion and Debate	13: "Not Knowing" is Your Friend 29: Understanding Discourse	89 204
Decision-Making Styles	18: A Bad Plan Poorly Executed 26: Leadership Styles for Decision Making	110 174
Empowerment	18: A Bad Plan Poorly Executed	110
Ethical Dilemmas	35: Ethical Dilemmas	268
Exceptional Organizations	1: Introduction 20: "Why Do Exceptional Organizations Fail?"	1 117
Failure of Exceptional Organizations	20: "Why Do Exceptional Organizations Fail?"	117
Followership	4: Yes, Even in Business 9: Everyone a Leader 25: Leaders and Followers	52 73 158
Human Motivation	31: Human Motivation	225
Human Resources	19: Right Person/Right Job	114
Inspiration	6: To Be Exceptional 7: The Servant as Leader 8: Imagine and Inspire 25: Leaders and Followers	60 65 69 158

EXHIBIT 2.1   Subject Index

TOPIC	CHAPTER	PAGE
Leadership	4: Yes, Even in Business 7: The Servant as Leader 8: Imagine and Inspire 9: Everyone a Leader 18: A Bad Plan Poorly Executed 25: Leaders and Followers 26: Leadership Styles for Decision Making	52 65 69 73 110 158 174
Leadership Succession	7: The Servant as Leader 20: "Why Do Exceptional Organizations Fail?"	65 117
Management Process	10: "What Do I Want?" 27: The 7-Step Process	78 183
Meaning in Life	21: "Any Luck?"	121
Measuring Performance	10: "What Do I Want?" 27: The 7-Step Process 33: Working in Alignment	78 183 244
Meetings	11: The Much Maligned Meeting 28: Meeting Management	82 196
Mental Models	13: "Not Knowing" is Your Friend 30: Mental Models	89 210
Mission Statements	16: Talk is Cheap	103
Modifying Actions	10: "What Do I Want?" 27: The 7-Step Process 33: Working in Alignment	78 183 244
Moral Excellence	5: Nice Guys Finish Last 23: Values	52 141
Organizing Principles	1: Introduction 22: Vision-Driven	1 130
Paradigm Shift	30: Mental Models	210
Personal Transformation	5: Nice Guys Finish Last 17: Guidance from Ghandi 23: Values	54 107 141
Profits	14: Yes, Even for Non-Profits 15: "Maximizing Profits–Isn't That Our Job?" 22: Vision-Driven	93 96 130
Power	12: Survival of the Fittest 25: Leaders and Followers 26: Leadership Styles for Decision Making	85 158 174
Reality	7: The Servant as Leader 10: "What Do I Want?" 13: "Not Knowing" Is Your Friend 27: The 7-Step Process 30: Mental Models	65 78 89 183 210

EXHIBIT 2.1   Subject Index

SECTION
1

SECTION 1

CASE STUDY

OVERVIEW

The American Woodmark case study describes the experience of an organization in its attempt to become an exceptional enterprise. It demonstrates the many variables that impact the transition to a new structure and the necessity for leaders to remain committed to the desired outcome but flexible in their approach to getting there. The American Woodmark vignettes included in the essays and lessons which follow support and give flavor to this narrative.

3

AMERICAN WOODMARK

I cofounded American Woodmark in 1980 to purchase the kitchen cabinet business of Boise Cascade through a leveraged buyout. At the time, we had sales of $35 million and three manufacturing plants. The company went public in 1986. In 1989 we launched our "1995 Vision," which dramatically changed our strategic direction. The company's revenues grew to over $800 million prior to the most recent economic downturn, which for our industry began in 2006. I was the CEO from the company's startup until 1996, after which I served as Chairman until 2004 and as a director since. Although this narrative covers American Woodmark's entire history, the focus is upon the creation and execution of the 1995 Vision.

A CROSSROADS

In early 1988, I wrote a "White Paper" to our Board of Directors indicating that our company's strategy, which had fueled record sales and earnings since the early 1980s, would result in our demise if followed unchecked into the 1990s. The paper's foreboding was not so much its dire warning, but rather that it offered no plan to resolve our crisis, because I had none!

By most every measure, American Woodmark was a very successful company. We had sales of $130 million, superior financial results, seven manufacturing plants and eleven distribution centers stretching from Florida to California. We were the leading supplier of stock kitchen cabinets to the home-center industry, serving five of the top ten chains. Forty percent of our sales were to home centers, thirty-five percent to independent distributors, and the balance to builders. All sales were under the American Woodmark brand name. We offered a limited product selection of nineteen styles that were inventoried in the distribution centers for single kitchen delivery anywhere in the continental United States. At the time, no other cabinet company could match our capabilities in the areas of logistics, order entry, delivery or sales coverage. This success, however, masked a much darker reality. After being loyal fans, a good number of our customers were now aggressively seeking competitors who could potentially match our offering.

We had grown along with our home center accounts in the early and mid-1980s as they expanded from local to regional service areas. This was fortuitous initially, because we had no other customers in their respective regions. By the late 1980s, however, these home centers—and in particular The Home Depot and Builders Square—were expanding nationally and entering markets which we had long served with independent distributors. Where this happened, we immediately had a conflict with our distributors who had previously enjoyed an exclusive representation. Furthermore, the home centers also entered each other's geographical regions and began competing directly with one another. Faced with these conflicts, and seeing us as being unable or unwilling to resolve them, both distributors and home centers responded by looking for other stock cabinet lines to sell. Furthermore, it was clear that the pressure from customers to replace our offering would only intensify over time.

The obvious solution of offering multiple brands with unique styles to reduce conflicts appeared totally unfeasible, because the key to our strategy was to inventory a *limited* number of product lines in regional distribution centers for quick delivery. To store all the styles necessary to support multiple brands would require a huge investment in inventory and higher production and logistic costs *just to keep the sales we already had*. Wherever we looked to resolve our dilemma, I saw only doom.

THE VISION

During my senior year at Dartmouth College, I was unsure of what to do upon graduation. I reduced my options to a career in clinical psychology or one in business. I was pursuing my undergraduate degree in psychology, which I enjoyed. I was also exposed to business because my father had owned a small machine shop. Over spring break, I interviewed for positions in both disciplines. As luck would have it, I found nothing related to psychology, but I did find a job at a bank. Following the path of least resistance, I took the bank position. I found it quite rewarding, and after one year, I went back to Dartmouth to get my M.B.A. from the Amos Tuck School. Upon graduation in 1970, I joined Boise Cascade, a major forest products company. In 1974, I became the general manager of its kitchen cabinet business which Boise had acquired three years earlier.

The former owner of the cabinet division operated the business in a very hands-on manner and made virtually every important decision. For example, prior to his selling the business to Boise Cascade, the only financial employee in the company was a bookkeeper tasked with preparing all checks, each of which the owner signed personally. While this procedure worked well for him when the business was small, it did not work as the business grew.

When I took over, the operation was in disarray. My initial focus was on creating a rudimentary organizational structure, putting people into key management positions, and creating

necessary accounting and management polices and procedures. These efforts were soon overridden, however, by the
greater need to restructure the business in light of a deepen-
ing recession and competitive pressures. We reduced our factories from seven to three, putting hundreds of people out of
work. While on a rational level I believed that we were doing
the right thing, from an emotional perspective I felt a sense
of failure and powerlessness in that I was unable to protect
people for whom I felt responsible. The division lost money
from 1973 to 1975 but returned to profitability in 1976.

While I was leading the business for Boise Cascade, there
was a part of me that dreamed about running my own enterprise. Since my father ran his own business, I was exposed
to this possibility from an early age. Although most of my job
experience was working for others, I had brief stints of self
employment. I started as a kid calling on neighbors to shovel
snow or mow lawns. During my summer break at graduate
school, I wrote and sold computer programs. I had also used
some of my free time to research various disciplines—such
as organizational theory, philosophy, psychology and history—to better understand how best to create more effective
organizations.

In March, 1977, I organized my thoughts about organizational effectiveness around a series of questions, some of
which were:

KEY QUESTIONS

- What is the nature of successful organizations?

- How effectively do organizations utilize their people? How can this effectiveness be increased?

- Do people at all organizational levels find their jobs
  meaningful? How can we make them more so?

- What is the potential payback for an organization which has all of its people working at their best to achieve the overall purpose of the organization?

- What values and policies will assure that an organization performs in an excellent manner?

- To improve organizational effectiveness, where does one start: policies, strategies, goals, recruitment or training? What factors are critical?

- Can business organizations simultaneously be responsible to society, customers, owners and employees?

- What is the nature of organizations that fail?

- What characteristics are necessary for an organization to maintain a continuity of effectiveness over time past one effective leader to a succeeding one?

Out of my reflections, I created a vision of an organization's culture that might embody the highly effective organization that I was seeking. I defined this cultural vision as:

A CULTURE WHERE:

- The organization prospers and grows

- The individual prospers and grows

- The actions of both the organization and the individual in pursuit of prosperity and growth are mutually reinforcing

- All parties with which the organization interacts benefit from their interaction

- The culture is strong enough to prosper and grow beyond the generation of leadership which initiated it.

I saw this vision as a framework for structuring individual and organizational effectiveness applicable to any type of enterprise.

In the summer of 1977, Boise Cascade engaged a major consulting firm to evaluate its building-products businesses, including the cabinet division. As a result of this study, it became clear to me that our division would be unable to grow as quickly as necessary to ever be of significance to Boise. Eventually, it would exit the business. While this study was being conducted, I approached my boss and indicated that if Boise did not want to retain the business, I would like to form a company to acquire it. His response was that, unless I had a lot more money than he thought I did, I should forget the idea.

THE JOURNEY

THE ACQUISITION: I now had a vision of buying the cabinet division and, in spite of my boss's negative reaction, I did not follow his advice and forget the idea. About one year later, I again approached him, indicating an interest in buying the business. However, I stated that if this were not feasible, I intended to leave the organization after a one-year transition period that would allow Boise Cascade to find someone to replace me. At this point, Boise had no interest in selling the business to me, but my action did prompt an active attempt to sell the business to others. While Boise pursued this effort, I prepared a business plan in the event that their effort proved unsuccessful. I researched ways to acquire companies by utilizing a large amount of borrowed money and relatively little equity. At the time, this process was known as "boot-strap financing." It later became known as "leveraged-buyout financing" in the 1980s and "private-equity financing" today. I sent articles on the subject to my boss to show him that such an acquisition was feasible.

By September 1979, Boise Cascade was unable to find a suitable buyer. I received a phone call indicating that Boise might be receptive to me presenting an acquisition proposal. Three of the division's key managers joined me as cofounders of a new company to buy the business. Al Graber, who led sales and marketing, joined the division in 1976 after having spent a number of years with Boise in various leadership roles. Jeff Holcomb, chief financial officer, came from outside of Boise in the same year after serving in accounting and finance positions with several manufacturing organizations. Don Mathias, the operations manager, had started with the division's predecessor company in the mid-1960s. He worked his way through virtually all of the organization's functional areas. The four of us came to an agreement with Boise and completed the acquisition on May 1, 1980.

In the formation of the new company, a key consideration of mine was the structuring of its ownership among the four founders. To determine the number of shares to offer each person, I considered not only their relative responsibilities, but also the way in which voting power, and therefore the legal control of the company, would be distributed. I deliberately structured the share distribution so that I together with any of the other three would have voting control, but that the other three acting together could out vote me and take charge. While I would be the CEO, they had the assurance that if they acted together, they could veto any of my initiatives. They could fire me if they feared that I was taking the company in the wrong direction. I remember sitting in my living room at home explaining to my would-be cofounders how the voting power would work. At no time since then did this subject ever come up.

The new company was called American Woodmark Corporation. Our four founders owned 85 percent of the stock, and a venture capital firm had a note convertible into the remaining 15 percent. The purchase price was $15.4 million, which was funded with equity capital of $350,000 and debt for the remainder including a subordinated note to Boise Cascade of $4 million. The debt was secured by the assets of the company, which included three manufacturing facilities. Over the preceding twelve months, the business had sales of $35 million and had earned a small operating profit. Sales were declining, however, because of a nationwide drop in new home construction and kitchen remodeling, both the result of rapidly rising interest rates. During the decade of the 1970s, housing starts had averaged 1.7 million per year. By May 1980, housing starts had dropped to an annual rate of less than one million, and the prime rate had skyrocketed to 19 percent. The annual interest rate paid to our primary lender was over 22 percent. Even though we were very concerned about the economic climate, none of us hesitated to go forward. We all believed that this was a once in a lifetime opportunity, and we were just glad to be in business.

STARTUP: When we acquired the business, we were prepared for a recession. However, we did not anticipate that it would be as deep or as long-lasting as what actually transpired. Our sales declined, and within a few months we were operating at a loss. By the start of 1981, because our initial equity investment was small, we had a negative net worth, meaning that our total liabilities exceeded our assets. Our loan structure had anticipated this possibility, and we still had additional cash we could borrow. But there was no sign of an improvement in the economy, and our cash availability would not go on forever. Although we had previously made a number of cost reductions, we took the additional step of operating in what we called a "survival mode." This meant that our primary focus was to assure that the company would stay in business over the short term. We eliminated everything but the most essential spending. When sales continued to fall in 1981 and 1982, we laid off additional hourly and salaried employees. At our lowest point, we had a negative net worth of $1.7 million. Although we still had borrowing capacity under our loan agreement, our primary lender had the power to shut down our business, or make other demands, on a moments notice. The difficult choices we had to make and the reality that we did not know when the recession would end led to many sleepless nights.

A NEW DIRECTION: 1980-1988: The markets for kitchen cabinets were divided geographically according to how they were served. In the Northeast, Mid-Atlantic and Midwest, cabinets were produced by regional or national manufacturers who reached the market through a network of independent distributors who purchased cabinets in trailer-load quantities for resale. We had a good network of distributors in these regions. However, in the South and West, local shops produced cabinets, delivering them in single-kitchen quantities to builders, kitchen dealers, lumber yards and area home centers. Since there were few independent distributors in these regions, our sales had been minimal.

In mid-June 1980, the regional sales manager of a major competitor approached us with what was for us a bold and radical idea. In less than a week, we committed to his plan and by August of that year, just three months after the company's startup, we opened our own captive distribution center in Atlanta to serve the same markets served by local cabinet shops. One of the home centers we serviced was a new company called The Home Depot which at the time had four stores. We sold single kitchens, delivering them on a weekly basis. Fortunately, we were soon successful with this approach—a direction that has driven our strategy ever since.

While we had the wisdom and courage to take advantage of this opportunity, we were fortunate to have it in the first place. Prior to contacting us, the regional sales manager had approached another cabinet company which was his first choice. That company's owner said, however, that he could not meet until after he had completed a fishing trip. By then, we had reached an agreement. Who knows how our future would have unfolded had this person not gone fishing.

We opened our second distribution center in Dallas in 1981, which along with the Atlanta operation, helped us weather the 1980-1982 recession. With an improved economy from 1983 to 1988, the home center industry grew very rapidly as local chains expanded into geographic regions and then nationally. Over this period, we added nine more distribution centers and expanded our sales organization to support the growing volume. We promoted Dave Blount to our senior leadership team to lead our manufacturing operations. Dave had joined us in 1976 upon the completion of his MBA and had quickly worked his way up through the organization. We added four factories supporting a fourfold volume gain. In 1986, we took the company public, providing funds for expansion and liquidity for equity holders.

CULTURAL CHANGE: 1980-1988: From 1980-1982, our primary focus was survival. From 1983-1988, it was to support our customers as they expanded dramatically. Whatever culture we created as a startup company evolved informally based primarily upon the behavior of our senior leadership team. This mechanism worked reasonably well when we had only three manufacturing locations, and all of us were readily visible throughout the organization. However, as we started adding distribution centers and additional manufacturing facilities, our personal reach was spread thin.

In 1986, we created a mission statement to codify the values, beliefs and behaviors we expected of our people. The statement focused on four key values described as follows:

- **Customer satisfaction**—Providing the best possible quality, service and value to the greatest number of people. Doing whatever is reasonable, and sometimes unreasonable, to make certain that each customer's needs are met each and every day.

- **Integrity**—Doing what is right. Caring about the dignity and rights of each individual. Acting fairly and responsibly with all parties. Being a good citizen in the communities in which we operate.

- **Teamwork**—Understanding that we must all work together if we are to be successful. Realizing that each individual must contribute to the team to remain a member of the team.

- **Excellence**—Striving to perform every job in a superior way. Being innovative, seeking new and better ways to get things done. Helping all individuals to become the best in their jobs and in their careers.

We introduced the mission statement through a series of small meetings conducted across the organization by our senior leadership team. We were excited that the mission statement would encourage people at all levels to take action in what we thought would be the best interests of the company. Unfortunately, after much fanfare, the statement had little impact. In a survey conducted in 1989 questioning how well the organization lived up to its mission statement values, managers throughout the company gave only "integrity" a high rating. They rated the other three values—"customer satisfaction," "teamwork" and "excellence" as deficient. Furthermore, they stated that there had been little progress made in acting according to these values since the mission statement was published.

The reality was that all of our energy was placed upon physically growing the business. We not only missed the longer-term strategic implications of our strategy, but we also neglected to create the cultural infrastructure necessary to sustain our growth. We gave only lip service to our stated values, relying upon only a few informal processes and procedures in their support. Although effective when we were smaller, our company had now become woefully inadequate, particularly as our competitors became more sophisticated.

THE 1995 VISION: Since the conflict among our various channels of distribution, described in the White Paper presented to our Board in 1988, had no recommended resolution, we set a goal for that year to better execute our existing plan. Our theme was "Back to Basics." Although there were a lot of basics that needed improvement, this was a little like building a sandcastle in the path of a steamroller. However, until we came up with a resolution to our strategic dilemma, there was nothing more to do. I wrestled anxiously with this dilemma for several months.

Finally, in August of 1988, we got a lucky break. A customer suggested that I read a just-released *Harvard Business Review* article written by George Stalk of the Boston Consulting Group titled, "Time—The Next Source of Competitive Advantage." Before completing the article, I had the answer to how I believed we could be a viable company once again.

In the article, Stalk showed how Japanese industry shifted its strategic focus at least four times since 1945. At first, they competed with *low-wage rates*. But by the early 1960s, when these were no longer an advantage, they developed *scale-based strategies* to reduce costs with large-volume capital-intensive facilities. By the mid-1960s, they introduced a third source of competitive advantage—the *focused factory*. With a focused factory, a company competed by offering a reduced product offering, frequently serving only the highest volume segments of a market—this was American Woodmark's strategy. The focused factory, however, could not effectively provide high variety if that were needed. This was our dilemma. To resolve such dilemmas, the Japanese introduced a fourth source of competitive advantage, the *flexible factory*.

Toyota led the development of the flexible-factory system. It relied upon *just-in-time* (JIT) production—where small quantities of materials were produced just prior to use in the next operation; *total quality control;* and *employee decision making* on the factory floor. By the mid-1970s, many Japanese firms were using these techniques.

Stalk included flexible manufacturing, increasing the rate of innovation and response time reduction of critical activities, as examples of using time as a source of competitive advantage. The article caused me to rethink many of the basic assumptions I held about how to run a manufacturing business. I arranged to meet with Stalk, where I confirmed my understanding of his principles and their relevance to American Woodmark.

I spent the next six months attempting to persuade my senior leadership team that we needed to turn the company upside down and embark on a radically new strategy. This was not an easy sell. Initially, none of them believed that our current situation was as bad as I thought it was. They thought my proposed solution seemed, at best, a pipe dream and, at worst, a nightmare. In the end, however, we all concluded that we needed to pursue this direction. In the spring of 1989, we presented our plan to the Board and received its approval. The key elements of the new strategy were as follows:

- **Multiple brands**—to create separate brands with unique product styles for independent distributors and key home center accounts

- **Product variety**—to expand the number of unique styles within each brand, increasing the total number of lines produced to over 100, resulting in *a five-fold increase*

- **Product innovation**—to be a product innovation *leader* within the cabinet industry where we had been a follower with our previous strategy

- **Distribution centers**—to eliminate all eleven distribution centers, shipping orders from our three regional assembly plants for delivery within the *same lead times* as existed with the centers

- **Manufacturing**—to *produce to customer order,* using JIT production techniques, rather than to inventory as previously done, and

- **New management processes**—to adopt new management techniques to change our existing culture as necessary to implement the above actions.

We called this our "1995 Vision" because we expected it to take us six years to complete. While the strategy's potential benefits were huge, so were its risks. It entailed a complete reorientation of how we ran the business with new operating philosophies and processes in virtually every part of the company. Second, we had to orchestrate many of the changes simultaneously because functional areas were interdependent. Third, the costs for introducing new products, phasing out distribution centers, and starting new operations were substantial. Fourth, there was the nagging question as to whether the benefits of JIT and other time-based operating techniques would actually be as great as expected. And fifth, there was the fear that as a public corporation, any disruption of our then favorable financial performance would significantly impact our stock price and shareholder value.

With all of these risks, one may wonder why we pushed ahead. Once I became aware of our situation, my motivation was quite simple—raw fear! I truly believed that if we followed the track we were on, American Woodmark would not only fail to become the company we aspired to be, but our very survival would be in jeopardy. Like people jumping from a burning building, our senior leadership team eventually saw that the anticipated strategy was our only way out. Furthermore, I had every confidence that we would pull this off, even if we were to hit a few speed bumps along the way.

We introduced the new strategy to our next level of management at a momentous meeting held at the Wayside Inn in Middletown Virginia in April, 1989. The news stirred everyone's deepest emotions, but the specific emotions felt were quite mixed. Our sales and marketing team, who had borne the front-line battle scars of our customers' wrath over market conflicts, were ecstatic that we were finally taking action to correct this situation. The additional brands and product lines were just what they needed. Our logistics and manufacturing teams, however, were simply in a state of shock. Not in their wildest dreams could they imagine our wanting to change so radically, when from their perspective, things were going so well. We were after all still setting performance records. Our logistics people saw us dismantling a nationwide distribution system that they had spent ten years creating. Meanwhile, our manufacturing team considered it literally impossible for us to achieve the stated product variety and delivery goals. They believed that the only hope for the company would be if the strategy's implementation were to get bogged down and eventually abandoned. With these varying sentiments, we plunged ahead.

The strategic plan we presented to our Board showed a slow growth in sales and profits over the implementation period. My intent was to orchestrate the transition so that one-time costs and disruptions would be spread out enabling us to still show some financial improvement each year. I believed the six-year horizon would give us the time to do this.

Our first initiative was to create a new brand of cabinets for the independent-distributor channel. A task force worked feverishly for one year to introduce the new brand, Timberlake, at the National Kitchen and Bath Show in the spring of 1990. The offering was a combination of existing and new door styles. For high-volume standard lines, we simply changed the labels of our existing products. But, we did add over 20 new and unique higher-grade styles, more than doubling the total offering from the existing American Woodmark line. We were quite proud of the result. Unfortunately, our distributors did not share our enthusiasm. The conversion costs for them to take on the line would be substantial. They would need to replace inventories, kitchen displays and marketing materials, plus forego whatever local brand equity they had created by marketing the American Woodmark name. Furthermore, they did not know if we were really committed to the new brand. If they were to incur the cost of making a change, perhaps they should replace us with a product line from a competitor who would be "truly committed to the needs of the distributor."

After several years of rapid growth, our sales dropped slightly in 1990. In addition to the lukewarm reception of the Timberlake brand, the economy had entered a recession. With the costs of developing the new lines and the manufacturing inefficiencies of more than doubling our product offering, our earnings dropped significantly. For the year, we were only marginally profitable. One year into the conversion, and we were already off track!

While our sales and marketing team had remained enthusiastic over this period, the atmosphere within our manufacturing and logistic groups was one of grudging compliance. The conviction remained that any slowing of the transition would help "save the company." Aware of these sentiments and struggling financially, we entered 1991 intent on slowing the pace of change and digesting what we had already done. Our sales continued to drop, and we were soon losing money. We reduced our planned new offerings to only a few lines to help stabilize the business. Then on Monday, March 4th, I received two phone calls. Coincidentally, our two largest home centers, The Home Depot and Builders Square, had each decided to add a second core supplier of stock cabinets. Suddenly, we faced the possibility of losing 50 percent of our volume with each account. The primary reason for their decisions was the increasing conflict with the "American Woodmark" brand as they expanded into each other's local markets. Secondarily, with our focus on creating new door styles for the Timberlake distributor brand, we had delayed improvements to our home center standard-style offering, which had become stale.

Our business was suddenly in crisis. We were already in a recession, operating our manufacturing plants on reduced schedules, losing money and struggling with the changes already made. The customer-conflict issue was even more critical than we had imagined, and now our home center sales were about to take a free fall. We were facing a moment of truth!

Our senior leadership team held what became an historic meeting in mid-March to address our situation. At a critical point in the meeting, we concluded that we needed to draw a line in the sand and do whatever it took to restore the leadership position previously held with our key home center accounts. We left the meeting resolved to do so. We committed to creating a separate brand of cabinets for Builders Square, thereby eliminating the conflict with Home Depot, who would retain the American Woodmark brand. We also committed to redesigning our highest-volume, standard door styles, which represented 70 percent of our existing volume, and to offering unique styling for most styles offered for each brand. To accomplish this would require that we quickly double our product offering, to over 100 lines! We finalized this plan in August, 1991 and began the implementation for a spring 1992 introduction. We had nine months to pull it off.

In sharp contrast to its initial response to the 1995 Vision, this time the entire organization put its full weight behind this initiative. With our best customers reducing our representation in their stores, the magnitude of our deteriorating market position was dramatically apparent to all. Now everyone in our organization was gripped with fear. Where our manufacturing team had collectively said that we were changing too fast, I can clearly recall one plant manager saying to me, "Tell us what you need and when you need it. We don't know how we will get it done, but we *will* get it done." We expanded factories, incurred huge marketing, product development and manufacturing start-up costs, pieced together new systems to handle the explosion in product variety and continued the gradual elimination of distribution centers.

By the following spring, we achieved what had previously seemed "impossible." At the Kitchen and Bath Show, we again showcased our new product offering. This time the impact was dramatic. Our distributors saw that we had upgraded their standard cabinet styles and gained confidence that the Timberlake brand would be around in the future. The separate brand for Builders Square reduced conflicts among home centers, and the updated product styles for all home center accounts enabled us to refurbish displays and generate excitement at the store level for our new offering. Our sales continued to decline in 1992 but turned upward by the end of the year with strong momentum going into 1993. We still lost significant position with our home center accounts, but we had stemmed the tide and gradually started gaining back market share.

The crisis was over, but we had paid a heavy price. We lost over $4 million for the year, down by $11 million from a record profit of over $7 million in 1989. Our stock price sank to a low of $1.25 from a 1989 high of $6.13.

It took us until 1996 to complete the 1995 Vision. We were successful in achieving all of its major strategic elements. We expanded from one brand of cabinets to four. We increased the product styles offered from 19 to over 100, doing in three years what our manufacturing team had thought would be impossible in six. We became a product development leader where we had previously been a follower. With our just-in-time manufacturing orientation, we eliminated eleven distribution centers and reduced finished-goods inventory from 250,000 units to less than 20,000, even though product variety and sales volume increased substantially. Delivery times to customers out of factories stayed the same as they had been from our distribution centers. Our on-time complete shipments rose to an outstanding performance level and product quality improved dramatically. Furthermore, we regained the confidence of our customers. We reestablished our leadership position in the stock segment of the home-center industry. With the Timberlake brand we became one of the leading suppliers to the distributor-builder market segment. Our journey did not follow the relatively straight path projected in 1989. It took us longer than expected, and we got severely bruised along the way.

CULTURAL CHANGE: 1989-1995: To be a product innovator offering expanded variety and multiple brands, we needed to make a greater number of decisions more quickly throughout the organization. The just-in-time manufacturing approach, where all activities were based upon producing to customer order rather than to inventory, necessitated our achieving substantially higher quality and on-time-complete delivery performance standards. It also required that we work in cells comprised of work teams, in which each team member had to complete a number of previously independent job functions.

To accomplish these strategic imperatives, we actually did have to live up to the stated values of our mission statement—to provide *customer satisfaction*, act with *integrity*, *work in teams* and in fact be *excellent*. Our people needed to be responsible, accountable, disciplined, flexible, creative thinkers as well as doers. They required skills not only in expanded job functions, but also in decision-making, communications and interpersonal relations. However, none of these capabilities existed to a sufficient degree at the time.

To create a new culture that would encompass these characteristics, we needed to establish new processes for product development, order entry, JIT manufacturing, quality and kitchen delivery. While the mechanics of these processes were relatively straightforward, the challenge was in getting our people to accept the magnitude of the changes required. They needed to give up old habits, embrace new ones and learn new skills and behaviors.

In 1989, we initiated several pilot-team programs in our manufacturing plants and trained our people in various new skills, such as simplifying work flows, reducing cycle times, lowering inventory levels and eliminating defects. We used outside consultants to design these programs, and in some instances to lead them. My hope was that the pilot programs would be so successful that others in the organization would naturally want to participate.

Unfortunately, after a two-year attempt, the pilot programs failed. The teams typically didn't have the understanding or support either from people higher up in the organization or from those in other departments with whom they interacted. Instead of small fires spreading rapidly, our pilot teams became small fires quickly snuffed out.

In 1991, with the help of another consultant, we introduced a cultural vision of *continuous improvement* whereby all employees would learn to "make decisions in the best interests of the company." We communicated this vision across the organization. We also established more than thirty new cross-functional teams comprised of people from different functional areas, each sponsored by a senior manager. In addition, fifty natural work groups, consisting of people who normally worked together, became "Daily Improvement Process" (DIP) teams empowered to suggest ideas and implement them within their work areas. Finally, we established an in-house training and development department and designated several full-time facilitators to assist in training and team development. Outside consultants were used primarily for concept development and the training of our own facilitators—not for implementation.

Although these efforts generated some significant performance improvements, they created problems of their own. Many of the cross-functional teams proposed solutions were not in step with the overall priorities of the company. DIP teams lacked momentum once easy to implement changes were completed, and people who were not yet involved in the process expressed frustration that they were not included.

In mid-1992, we called a "time out" to assess where we were. We decided to start over. Our senior leadership team concluded that using a somewhat "canned" management process brought to us by outside consultants was not a good fit for our organization. We needed a tailored program that would take into account our culture as it existed at the time and as we wanted it to become. We concluded that I would write four lessons to be delivered to all employees on a "level-to-level" basis, where, starting at the top of the management hierarchy, supervisors would teach lessons to those who worked directly for them and who would, in turn, teach their own direct reports until eventually everyone in the organization would be taught each lesson. The lessons included a standardized process for doing work, essential communication skills, an exercise modeling teamwork and continuous improvement and a methodology for developing client-provider relationships.

We had originally anticipated that it would take six months to complete the training. It actually took three years. We found that people enjoyed the lessons but then went quickly back to their prior techniques and methodologies without changing their behavior. We called another time out to assess the situation. We concluded that before teaching a lesson to a lower level, the higher level team first had to exhibit that the core-training principles were actually practiced. We created internal advisors drawn from different areas of the organization who conducted workshops for each team and assessed their mastery of the principles.

Gradually, the training worked its way through the organization and behaviors began to change. People took greater ownership in their job responsibilities and spent time thinking about how best to do an activity rather that just doing it as they had done it in the past. We saw many small actions initiated in teams generating significant improvements in quality, safety, delivery, cost and other performance targets.

The level-to-level training became one of two mechanisms that together were the most instrumental in creating our desired cultural change. The second one was initiated in 1993 and consisted of a five-day leadership retreat. Each session was limited to twenty-four participants, who came from the managerial and professional ranks across the organization. I wrote most of the lessons and taught the class for each of the five days. I was joined each day by a separate member of senior management who participated in the training. The lessons included topics ranging from decision-making and planning to meeting management, leadership styles, teamwork, values, methods of discourse, cultural change and methods for resolving ethical dilemmas. Each class was divided into three teams which did special projects, and the evenings were spent in dialogue sessions and story telling.

Participants left these sessions, not only with specific knowledge and skills but, more importantly, with a heightened sense of the purpose of the company, its values and the roles they could play as part of the organization and its future. For some, the sessions were transformational to their personal lives, enhancing their relationships with spouses and children. With the success of the first retreat, we conducted four more in 1994 and two in 1995. We had a total participation of one hundred fifty people or more than twenty-five percent of our total salaried workforce. As more and more people completed the level-to-level training, the leadership retreats and the training for the various other programs and processes we had initiated, we gradually reached a critical mass that tipped the organization toward our desired culture.

Training in new processes was a critical element that enabled the vast majority of our people to achieve the higher performance expectations of our new strategy and culture. However, even with this, not all people were capable of meeting these standards and had to be separated from their prior positions. While we made every effort to find other more appropriate positions within the company, in cases, especially for those higher up in the management hierarchy, separation from the company was the only alternative. This was particularly difficult where people had performed well relative to the organization's past expectations.

By 1995, we had created a culture that met, at least to a minimum degree, the needs of our 1995 Vision and our mission statement values of *customer satisfaction, integrity, teamwork* and *excellence.* Although it would be a continuing challenge, we had for the most part the *right people* in the *right jobs.* Our people now had not only the basic education, training and tools that enabled them to do their existing jobs well but also an orientation toward making improvements and adopting necessary change. We were ready for the next step in the company's evolution.

1996 TO THE PRESENT: In 1996, Jake Gosa replaced me as CEO, serving until 2007. Jake had joined the company in 1991 as our Vice President of Sales and Marketing. In 2007, Kent Guichard, who had joined us in 1993 as our Chief Financial Officer, succeeded Jake as CEO. While the company's history under their respective reigns is each a story in itself, I will briefly summarize this period.

The 1995 Vision created a strategic and cultural platform which we could build upon for the future. The home center industry continued to consolidate with only two major players remaining, The Home Depot and Lowe's. American Woodmark emerged as the primary provider of stock kitchen cabinets to both of these accounts. Our position with these two entities together with the expansion of our Timberlake builder program enabled us to become a growth company gaining significant market share and establishing the economies of scale necessary to compete on a national level.

Our growth was supported by many new process improvements—a number of which were significant innovations within our industry. These included initiatives in product development, manufacturing, quality, customer service, delivery and management information systems. In the human resource arena, we established comprehensive programs in recruiting, employee orientation, performance planning and appraisal, employee development and succession planning. The five-day leadership training initiated in 1993 has continued with over 600 people attending since its inception.

American Woodmark's strategy has been to compete solely within the cabinet industry, realizing that our business is cyclical and that recessions are likely every seven to eight years. We have accepted this eventuality and have prepared for it by building significant cash reserves with the intent of weathering whatever storm might blow our way. The housing industry peaked in 2006 and dropped precipitously since. Although our volumes were down substantially and we lost money, we maintained a strong cash reserve, gained market share and enhanced our competitive posture coming out of the downturn.

RESULTS

As shown in Exhibit 3.1, sales for American Woodmark have risen from $30 million in 1981 to a peak of over $800 million prior to the most recent housing downturn. Income has grown with the exception of three periods when we lost money during severe economic recessions. Currently, assets total more than $250 million and shareholder equity is in excess of $130 million and the company has returned to profitability. Exhibit 3.2 presents the company's financial strength, where cash-on-hand of over $70 million now exceeds total debt of less than $25 million. The company is the third largest cabinet manufacturer nationally and the industry leader in the stock-segment category.

Although the organization has made difficult choices in the downturn, including layoffs and plant closings, we have maintained a highly valued relationship with employees. This relationship has been supported by our being very candid about the company's reality and by dealing with employees with respect, integrity and a sense of caring. Key cus-

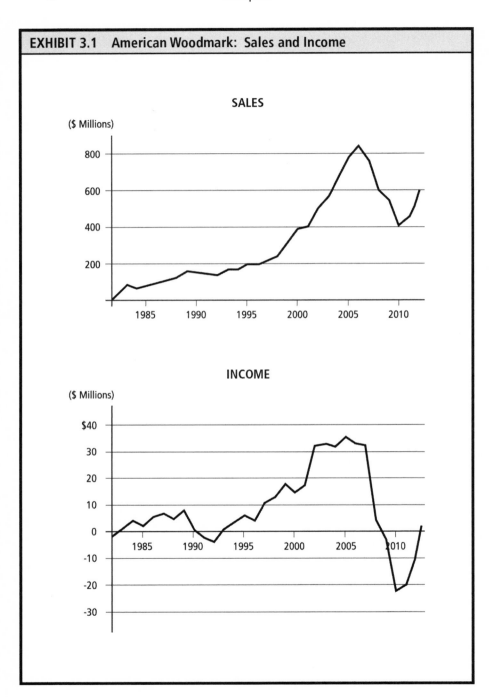

EXHIBIT 3.1   American Woodmark: Sales and Income

SALES

($ Millions)

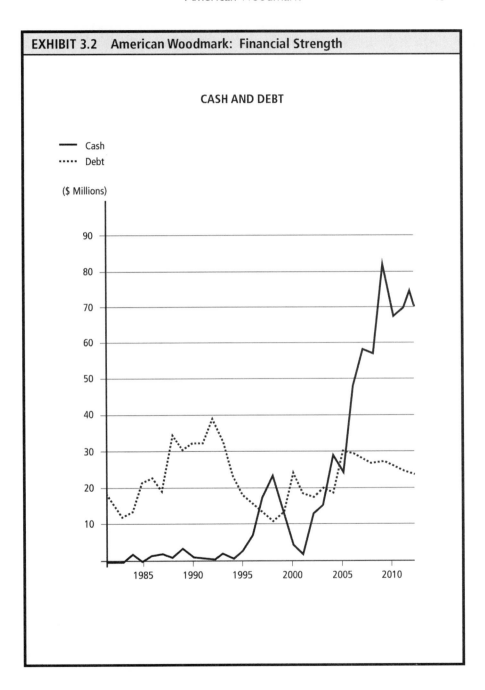

EXHIBIT 3.2   American Woodmark: Financial Strength

CASH AND DEBT

tomers and suppliers view the company more as a partner than as a traditional buyer and seller of goods, and we work to be good citizens in our communities. Our stock price has increased from a low $1.25 per share in the 1990-1992 recession to above $25 per-share coming out of the most recent recession.

While a cultural vision is something to aspire to, I don't believe that it can ever be fully achieved. American Woodmark has performed reasonably well relative to the culture I envisioned in 1977 and the mission statement we established in 1986. We are reminded of this when new hires reflect favorably upon our culture in comparison to those of organizations where they had previously worked.

In summary, American Woodmark is *viable* in that we achieve our purpose of effectively providing kitchen and bath cabinets to the American family; *sustainable* as evidenced by two highly successful CEO transitions, a strong financial posture and a substantial long-term competitive advantage; and *valued* in that we provide superior returns to our various stakeholders.

REFLECTIONS

THE STORY: In his book, *The Black Swan* Nassim Nicholas Taleb states that we give meaning to what we experience by creating logical cause-and-effect narratives to explain what are often random events. This is certainly evident with the American Woodmark story. Although I have attempted to describe the elements of chance that related to key turning points in our company's strategic direction—such as our entry in 1980 into the home center and builder-direct markets and the creation of our 1995 Vision, I have not included many of the missteps, misunderstandings of reality, impacts of every day experiences and the unknowable and uncontrollable events that helped shape our history. For example, we acquired two small cabinet companies, which because they failed, were not included in the narrative. However, together they influenced our mindset to stick with our knitting and grow organically rather than through further acquisitions. Also missing are the many errors we made in hiring senior executives who proved unsuccessful and whom we later replaced.

RISK: The level of financial risk—as measured by American Woodmark's cash availability and debt-to-equity ratios—played a key role in our history. The only way that I and my cofounders could possibly *create* American Woodmark was by our willingness to assume an extremely high level of risk, as evidenced by our 45-to-1 debt-to-equity ratio at the time of our startup. Once American Woodmark was created, however, a priority was to *sustain* the business, so it became imperative that we reduce our financial risk to a safe level as soon as feasible. We were very *lucky* in our early years that there were no negative events that we were unable to absorb. By 2006 we had established significant cash reserves and a very low debt-to-equity ratio of 1-to-5. Our financial strength enabled us to successfully survive a dramatic *unlucky* event, the 60 percent drop in our industry's volume from peak to trough from 2006-2009.

VISION AND ACTION: While uncontrollable events—or luck—certainly played a role in our history, there were, however, aspects of the narrative that I believe do demonstrate cause-and-effect experiences. From its inception, I wanted American Woodmark to become the "best-run" company in the cabinet industry. I wasn't focused upon a particular sales or earnings target. Rather, I wanted the company to be *among* the industry leaders in total revenues and to be the *best overall* when multiple metrics, such as quality, service, customer care, profitability and shareholder returns, were considered. Being the best also meant having a culture of the highest values, where our people could "prosper and grow."

Over time the above conception was codified: first, with the creation of our mission statement in 1986; second, with successive six-year visions beginning with our 1995 Vision and third, with leadership training that incorporated many of the ideas described in the essays and lessons of this book. Although given further shape, the essence of what was originally pictured remained intact.

While we held firm to the primary elements of our vision, the actions we took to achieve them changed continually. This was a reflection of both the changing environment we lived in and the reality that the actions we took were often inadequate. Although I don't know whether our batting average for decision-making was any better than other organizations, I do believe that *holding fast* to our vision and making *timely* corrections to actions that did not support it were key factors in our success.

LEADING IN GOOD TIMES AND BAD: I found that choosing a proper direction was easier in tough times—resources were limited, choices were fewer and people wanted to see the organization take action, even if painful, because they feared the status quo. On the contrary, in good times there were more resources, more choices and people resisted change because they were comfortable with where they were. In good times the right choices were not obvious, and there was often a danger of taking the organization in the wrong direction.

While decision-making was easier in tough times, the emotional challenge was not. I thought it imperative that I project confidence and optimism to those with whom I engaged, even when in actuality I did not feel that way. I was conscious that people continually monitored my "mood," and if they saw a crack in my facade, they might panic, thinking that "if he is worried, then I should be really worried." When I did falter, word would get back to me of comments such as, "What's wrong with Bill?"

In tough times, people had an emotional need to see quick results from actions taken. Unfortunately, there were often significant lags between actions and outcomes. Even if actions taken were excellent, no one felt good if operating results were poor, especially if we were losing money. Convincing people to be patient and stay the course became a continuing challenge.

Early in my career I felt a paternalistic responsibility to protect employees from bad outcomes. As mentioned in the narrative, I felt a sense of failure and remorse when I was unable to do so. Eventually I realized that the employees had responsibility for their own lives and that, rather than trying to protect them from the harshness of reality, my responsibility was to help them live through it. We did this by giving employees timely information about the status of their jobs, treating them with respect, and helping them as best we could through transitions.

It was easy for me to remain grounded and humble when times were tough but not when they were good. For example, during the mid-1980s, our senior management team and I assumed that our leadership position in the home center segment was somewhat invulnerable, when in fact our competitors were gaining on us and preparing for us to falter—which we eventually did. This event was a painful but good learning experience. Since then, I attempted to be vigilant against letting hubris set in, either for me or for those around me.

YOUR STORY: By sharing the American Woodmark story, I do not mean to imply that it should be a template for your organization's story. Rather it is intended to stimulate your thinking as to what is possible for you and your organization and what actions you may wish to consider for getting there. While each organization's circumstances are different, I believe the principles presented in this book will benefit any organization in its quest to become exceptional.

SECTION
2

SECTION 2

ESSAYS

OVERVIEW

This section presents a collection of essays on a range of subjects relevant to the creation of exceptional organizations. They are divided into four parts. "The Vision" describes what is possible for both exceptional organizations and the individuals within them. "The Leader" presents the leadership imperatives necessary to create and sustain exceptional institutions. These imperatives reflect the organizing principles of *inspiration* and *right person / right job*. "Processes and Tools" offers various beliefs and processes supporting the *vision-driven* and *value-based* organizing principles. "The Journey" shares the challenges that face those attempting to create such exceptional institutions.

Each essay includes "Questions for Reflection." These questions are intended to help readers relate the essay topic to their own experiences and to challenge their existing beliefs on the subject. Each essay is also cross-referenced to corresponding essays and lessons that relate to it.

SECTION 2.1

THE VISION

OVERVIEW

This section includes three essays that give the reader a picture of what is possible. The first, "Yes, Even in Business," promotes a vision combining individual and organizational self-interest with serving a higher cause and behaving according to society's highest values. The second, "Nice Guys Finish Last," provides a vision of moral excellence in which assertiveness and self-determination are not antithetical to caring and concern, but are two traits that can be embraced by the same individual. The third, "To Be Exceptional," presents an example of an exceptional organization and a methodology for creating one.

4

YES, EVEN IN BUSINESS

I believe we can create institutions—yes, even in business—that not only achieve the self-interests of members but also serve a greater good and act according to society's highest values.

Some years ago, I attended a five-day workshop where I was the only business person among psychologists, counselors and teachers. After the third day, one from the group came to me and said somewhat sheepishly, "We didn't know what to expect when we learned you were in business. You aren't that bad after all." I realized I had shaken one of their long-held beliefs about people in business. I did nothing, however, to challenge a second one: which was, because they thought their careers to be virtuous, so were they.

About this time I read Victor Frankl's classic—*Man's Search for Meaning*—where he shared his experience in Auschwitz. I was moved by his portrayal of a camp commander who used his own money to buy medicine for prisoners and of a guard who shared his bread rations with them. Frankl contrasted this behavior with the absolute brutality of some Capos, who were prisoners chosen by the camp authority to control fellow prisoners. Frankl concluded that people were decent or indecent regardless of where grouped in society.

Throughout my career I have been a student of organizations—large and small, simple and complex, for profit and non-profit. I would categorize them more by the character of their leadership than by the nature of their structures. Any structure may be oriented toward self-interest alone or a balance between individual needs and service to others. It is the leader who determines whether we have one orientation or the other.

But who determines who leads? The traditional view is that "leaders lead" and "followers follow," where who leads is based upon position or rank. If we define "leadership," however, as "the act of influencing people to follow a particular direction," then whenever we do so—regardless of our formal status—we become leaders. From this perspective, everyone is a leader and everyone a follower.

In any situation where two or more people come together, we can become the creators of our own communities—whether we are CEOs of corporations, leaders of non-profits, coaches of Little League teams, teachers with rooms full of third-graders, coworkers on a shipping dock or guards sharing bread with prisoners in a concentration camp.

Who determines whether we have an orientation toward self-interest alone or one that also serves a greater good? We do.

QUESTIONS FOR REFLECTION

- Have you experienced people who have behaved badly within institutions that you considered virtuous?

- Have you witnessed good behavior within organizations that you thought were morally unfit?

RELATED CHAPTERS

5

NICE GUYS FINISH LAST

Nice guys finish last—so goes the traditional wisdom. But being nice—that is, expressing a "concern for others"—does not mean being weak, a pushover or unassertive. On the contrary, depending upon the circumstances, the same individual can be tough, competitive and assertive as well as sensitive and caring. I believe that organizations that foster the moral development of their members, and thereby encourage the appropriate use of a range of behaviors, give their organizations a tremendous competitive advantage over those that do not.

I recall the very first time I presented a training module titled "Caring" to a management team at one of American Woodmark's manufacturing plants. After dinner that evening, we held a dialogue session with the group at which each person had the opportunity to comment on the training module or any other topic relevant to the company. One woman, full of emotion, related that she recently had a death in her family and that she was overwhelmed by the outpouring of support she received from the company and her coworkers. To her, this behavior spoke to what the company was all about.

In her book, *In a Different Voice,* Carol Gilligan describes three stages of moral development. The first is *survival,* when infants focus solely upon themselves and their own needs.

The second occurs in early childhood when children have a sense of both themselves and others. This stage is typically different for boys than for girls. Women in most societies are the primary care givers. Along with this responsibility comes the role of maintaining relationships in the family and the community. Girls identify with their mothers whom they see modeling these behaviors. For girls, the second stage of moral development is *caring*. They develop a sense of responsibility for others, cooperation, equality and community. Boys, in contrast, model their fathers, whom they see as going outside the family to hunt, fish or earn a paycheck. What is right is to stand on one's own and develop skills to impact the world. Boys realize that there are "others" and that they must distinguish themselves in comparison. For boys, the second stage of development is *identity*. They seek achievement, competition and higher relative positions. They value autonomy, independence and freedom. The formation of rules, the administration of justice and the concept of fairness become valued because they set guidelines for achieving these distinctions.

The third stage of moral development is *maturity,* whereby men and women both have a sense of *identity* and *caring.* Once a man achieves a separate identity his challenge is to see his behavior from another's perspective and to take responsibility for others as well as for himself. A woman, who in adolescence established a sense of caring, must learn that she has a separate identity, and that she is at least as worthy of care as someone else. At maturity both men and women embrace concepts that only one sex valued at stage two. These are *justice, caring, autonomy, equality, fairness, truth, connection, identity, freedom, achievement, independence* and *responsibility.*

In *The Soul of Corporate Leadership*, William J. O'Brien linked the development of high performing value-based organizations with the moral development of their leaders. He indicated that much of American industry is run by a command-and-control governance structure, in which leaders tell their subordinates what to do and then check to see if it is done.

O'Brien contrasts the command-and-control approach with a *value-based* structure, where the leader points out the direction, and the members find the best way to get there. With a command-and-control structure, what is important is "who" is in charge and actions are focused on pleasing the boss, not making a mistake and keeping one's job. While command-and-control may be effective in situations where all of the necessary knowledge is held by the leader, it is of lesser value in a complex world where no one individual has all the answers.

Entities which embrace command-and-control governance structures are "traditional organizations" as described in the Introduction. Their stakeholders pursue their own self-interests and relate to each other on a transactional basis of "value received for services rendered."

With a value-based orientation, the focus is upon whatever is in the best interests of the enterprise. In a value-based structure, work is organized not only to achieve specific tasks but also to serve the human need for purpose and the fulfillment of each member's potential. Stakeholders pursue both "self-interest" *and* "concern for others."

Value-based enterprises act according to universal human values. What is important is that organizational leaders and members not only embrace these values but also *practice* them even when there are motivations to do otherwise. O'Brien describes a goal of achieving *moral excellence,* which is the equivalent of Gilligan's description of moral maturity.

The phrase "nice guys finish last" has its philosophical underpinnings in the popular work of Ayn Rand, who in her book, *The Virtues of Selfishness* asserts that "*concern with his own interests* is the essence of a moral existence, and that man must be the beneficiary of his own actions."[1] Using Gilligan's nomenclature, Rand never reaches stage three of moral development. Rather she views stage-two *identity*—which equates to "the pursuit of self-interest"—as the highest moral value. From Rand's perspective *identity* is mutually exclusive with *caring*—or "concern for others," which she does not see as a value at all.

It is a fundamental premise of this book that *identity* and *caring*, or "self-interest" and "concern for others" are *not* mutually exclusive but rather are both elements of a range of values comprising the highest level of moral formation, as articulated by Gilligan and O'Brien. This premise is further supported by Riane Eisler, author of the landmark book, *The Chalice and the Blade.* Eisler describes two social systems that over the history of humankind have governed the range of human interactions from individuals to nation-states. The first, the *Dominator Model,* is comprised of rigid hierarchies, ranking—typically of men over women, competition, violence and command-and-control governance structures. The second, the *Partnership Model,* is characterized by flexible hierarchies, ranking by merit—while retaining formal hierarchal structures, the use of power to accomplish a task more so than power as control, equal status for men and women, nonviolence, mutual relationships and the embracement of both *identity* and *caring* as. Although the Dominator Model has governed social systems for most of human history, Eisler notes many instances where the Partnership Model has been predominate. The principles in this book are consistent with Eisler's Partnership Model.

American Woodmark went through its own cultural-change initiative to convert from a command-and-control to a value-based governance structure. We had one group of people who immediately welcomed this transition because the new approach fit their own sense of values, a second group who definitely would never adapt to the new culture and who would eventually leave the organization through their own volition or that of the company's and a third for whom it was unclear as to whether or not they could make the transition. As part of this cultural-change effort, as mentioned in the case study, we conducted a five-day leadership retreat for individuals with supervisory responsibility. The retreat was conducted by our senior leadership team in classes of twenty-four at a time. Over the years, more than 600 people attended this retreat. Two in particular stood out.

Jim had worked in the predecessor company to American Woodmark. I recall when I had first joined the company a plant manager told me that he used Jim to agitate the union representatives among the workers until they would be so intimidated that they would leave the organization. When Jim came to the retreat, I doubted that he would ever make the transition to the culture we desired. I could not have been more wrong. About a week after the class, someone came up to me and said, "What did you do to Jim?" Everyone who worked with him said that he came back from the retreat a new person, treating people with care and respect that he had rarely exhibited before.

Rick, who worked in a different factory, was very strong technically but was abrasive and demeaning to those who worked for him. He, too, appeared unlikely to adapt to the new culture, but like Jim he returned from the retreat a "new person"—so much so that his wife called his plant manager to thank him for sending Rick to the retreat and asked if she could attend a future session herself. In less than a week, Jim and Rick each went through personal transformations that changed their lives.

Organizations can foster their members' growth toward moral maturity. Those that achieve this status are neither "always nice" nor "always tough," but rather they choose behaviors that best fit the circumstances. In essence, they can play all of the keys on the piano to their own and their organizations' benefit. Yes, even nice people can finish first!

QUESTIONS FOR REFLECTION

● How do you see your own moral formation? How do your behaviors reflect your values?

● What is your organization's governance structure? How does it relate to the command-and-control and value-based structures presented here?

RELATED CHAPTERS

6

TO BE EXCEPTIONAL

I believe that we can create *exceptional organizations* that are viable, sustainable and valued—*viable* in that they achieve their missions and act according to society's highest values,—*sustainable*, by being viable over time and—*valued* in that all stakeholders benefit to a greater degree than they would with alternative entities. Exceptional organizations are characterized by inspiring visions, well-executed strategies for superior competitive advantage and positive cash flow, strong value-based cultures and the placement of the right people in the right jobs. Such organizations are exceptional because there are so few of them.

I attended a seminar some years ago on "the learning organization" led by Peter M. Senge, author of *The Fifth Discipline*. Exceptional organizations, as described here, have many characteristics in common with learning organizations as he defined them. Listening to Senge's presentation, it was clear that such entities would be vastly superior to traditional structures. During a break, I asked Senge how many organizations had achieved this status. He responded, "Very few." When asked why, he said, "Because it is so very hard to do."

Few leaders are even aware of the *possibility* of their organizations being exceptional, and fewer still are those who aspire to create such entities. For those who do, three criteria are preconditions for success. Leaders must have the requisite wills, skills, values and open mindedness. Second, they need the necessary resources to keep their organizations functioning until they create a competitive advantage that generates a sustainable cash flow. Finally, they need the support of whoever they are accountable to—owners, directors or others higher in their organizations' hierarchies.

For those organizations that meet these criteria, the task to create exceptional organizations is simple in concept. The first step is to create a clear vision of the desired organization. While this vision will be unique for each entity, it will include the "viable," "sustainable" and "valued" elements described above. The second step is to understand the organization's current reality relative to its desired state. Where there is a discrepancy between the two, the third step is to take action to move the current reality toward the organization's vision. Actions taken can be evaluated for results and modified as appropriate until the desired state is achieved.

While simple in concept, the execution of this endeavor is difficult in practice. Strategies for competitive advantage may be elusive. There will be resistance to change, false steps taken and the diversion of energy and resources to the immediacy of other priorities. To carry this effort to fruition requires a strong leader who will remain resolute in spite of these obstacles. Depending upon the size of the entity and the distance to be traveled, the transition may take not months but years.

At the seminar just mentioned, I also asked Senge if he could suggest someone I could talk to who had successfully made such a transition. He recommended a person from Hanover Insurance, William J. O'Brien—introduced in the preceding chapter as the author of *The Soul of Corporate Leadership*. O'Brien joined Hanover Insurance in 1971 to work for its CEO Jack Adams, who O'Brien then succeeded in 1979. At the time O'Brien joined Hanover, the company was ranked in the bottom of every industry comparison. The two set out to create what O'Brien called an organization of "unsurpassed excellence," which he said he couldn't define but which he would recognize when he saw it. O'Brien said that it took Hanover twelve years to achieve this vision. By 1991, upon his retirement, the company had reached the top of its industry rankings. Its earnings per-share were forty-times greater that they were in 1969. Although O'Brien said one could not put a number onto it, the atmosphere in the organization had gone from resignation, compliance and despair to engagement, commitment and hope.

At the time I met O'Brien, American Woodmark was struggling through the third year of a major organizational-change effort. We were behind on our performance expectations. We had missed key milestones, we were losing money, and to some, our ultimate success was in doubt. Hanover's results gave us a sense of what was possible. O'Brien provided support and good counsel and soon became a mentor to me and other members of our senior leadership team. He gave us the lift we needed to persevere.

Although the decision to undertake a major organizational transition cannot be taken lightly, given that the preconditions are met, there is a very good probability of success. For those who prevail, the creation of an exceptional organization is more than worth the challenges necessary to bring it into being.

QUESTIONS FOR REFLECTION

- What are the aspirations of your organization? Can you frame them in terms of it being "viable," "sustainable" and "valued?"

- What is the status of your organization today relative to the above characteristics?

- If your organization aspires to become exceptional, does it's leadership have in place the three preconditions for success?

RELATED CHAPTERS

SECTION 2.2

THE LEADER

This section presents three essays that explore leadership principles that impact the creation and maintenance of exceptional organizations. First, "The Servant as Leader" demonstrates that it is imperative that leaders put the mission and the well-being of their institutions ahead of their own personal gain. Second, "Imagine and Inspire" shows the power of inspiration relative to rewards and punishments as a source of motivation. Third, "Everyone a Leader" describes the extraordinary potential that can be released when all members of organizations see themselves as being either leaders or followers depending upon the situation.

7

THE SERVANT AS LEADER

I believe that for organizations to be exceptional, they need servant leaders at their helms—those who serve causes greater than their own self-interests and who inspire their members to do the same. Celebrity CEOs need not apply.

What do Ken Lay of Enron, Bernie Ebbers of Worldcom, and Dennis Koslowski of Tyco have in common? That's right. They were all included in a book published in 1999 that profiled the fifty "very best business leaders in America."[1] Not long after their inclusion, they were each found guilty of criminal behavior regarding their business conduct. The three were further distinguished in a 2008 article titled, "The Seven Most Crooked CEOs of All Time."[2]

While these three displayed some of the worst behavior, the public is continually outraged with headlines of other CEOs who negotiate unseemly compensation packages. The most egregious of these are those who have overseen the demise of their corporations, but who nevertheless have garnered outlandish exit pay or, if they stayed, "retention bonuses."

Such behaviors exemplify *self-focused leadership,* where the primary motivation is to serve one's own self-interests. For such leaders, acting in pursuit of their organizations' purposes is not an end in itself, but rather a means to an end. If they become celebrities, it is because they have created a focus upon themselves, rather than their organizations. Institutions led by such individuals are characterized by behaviors to "please the boss," where doing so garners rewards and failure to do so leads to punishments. While such behaviors are motivated, they are not inspired. Furthermore, pleasing the boss may have nothing to do with actually achieving an organization's purpose. Where this happens, behaviors are soon misaligned. Finally, self-focused leaders have little interest in grooming competent successors because any benefits of doing so would fall on someone else's watch.

Rarely is a different type of leader in the headlines. I first met one such individual at a hotel at Boston's Logan Airport. He had overseen the creation of a unique high-performing organization and, since his retirement, had worked as a consultant helping other organizations do the same. At the end of our discussion, I indicated that I would like to engage his services, but that I needed to wait until American Woodmark—which at the time was struggling through a severe recession—could afford them. He responded that he would work for us for free.

I have served as a director on several for-profit and nonprofit boards. During my tenures, there were five occasions where different CEOs declined higher pay when offered. In each instance, they were concerned that the higher compensation, or simply the receipt of a pay increase at all, was inappropriate given their organizations' circumstances at the time.

To describe behaviors such as these, Robert Greenleaf, in his book of the same title, coined the term *Servant Leadership*. Servant leaders are motivated to pursue causes greater than their own self-interests and when necessary make sacrifices to do so. Paradoxically, their orientation to serve rather than be served is completely counter to the popular perception of what leadership is about.

Jim Collins, in his bestseller, *Good to Great*, reinforces the importance of servant leadership when he characterizes the traits of corporations that successfully transformed themselves from being *good* performers within their respective industries to being *great*. Each of these organizations was led by what Collins calls a *level-5 leader*—"an individual who blends extreme personal humility with intense personal will."[3] Level-5 leaders fit the description of servant leadership in that their ego needs are channeled first and foremost to the institution, and not themselves.

Servant leaders are humble. They are good listeners and are more likely to seek the truth than assume they already know it. They are effective delegators and good mentors. They are also strong-willed and results-oriented. Organizations characterized by such leadership are more likely to have inspiring visions, better understanding of reality, greater alignment of behaviors in support of their visions, stronger results and better development of their people for the future.

Self-focused leadership and servant leadership are two ends of a spectrum. While many people have the potential to move up the spectrum toward greater servant leadership, there are others so egocentric that they cannot and never will.

The owner of the predecessor company to American Woodmark created a culture to "please the boss," in which self-focused leadership was the norm. Through selective hiring, promotions and either voluntary or involuntary departures, American Woodmark gradually created a culture of servant leadership. A first stage in this transition was the choice of cofounders of American Woodmark who fit the servant-leadership mold. A second, more conscious stage was the inclusion of *integrity*—doing what is right—as one of the four pillars of our mission statement adopted in 1986. Since *doing what is right* is almost synonymous with servant leadership, using "integrity" as a criterion for personnel decisions naturally led to the advancement of servant leadership and the discouragement of self-focused leadership. More recently, this transition has been further strengthened by

American Woodmark's formal employee performance and development systems. Employees are evaluated according to the dimensions of job performance and cultural fit with the company's mission statement and supporting values.

We can create cultures that foster servant leadership where those who have the potential for such behavior are nurtured and those who do not either quit or are asked to leave. While not the only step, a culture characterized by servant leadership is fundamental to the creation of exceptional organizations.

QUESTIONS FOR REFLECTION

● Have you witnessed examples of self-focused leadership? Of servant leadership?

● Where do you see yourself on the spectrum from self-focused leadership to servant leadership?

RELATED CHAPTERS

8

IMAGINE AND INSPIRE

I believe in rewards and punishments. I also believe that, while necessary, they are greatly overemphasized as a source of motivation. Better yet is to be inspired!

Organizations use rewards and punishments to control behavior, appealing to what its members want—money, recognition and advancement, or by avoiding what they don't want—less money, reprimands or job loss.

Effective rewards and punishments, such as compensation systems, scorecards and performance evaluations help align individual actions to what is best for the enterprise. The difficulty arises when these become the predominant or sole source of motivation.

When I was fifteen, my father took me to the movie *Spartacus*, the story of a slave in ancient Rome who led a rebellion of fellow slaves. While slave revolts were not uncommon, they were soon put down by Roman legionnaires. Under the leadership of Spartacus, however, his band of slaves overwhelmed local garrisons and regional forces, freed other slaves to expand their ranks and moved from Sicily northward toward the capital in Rome. Finally, the emperor brought to bear the full force of the Roman army and in a climactic battle crushed the slave forces. After the battle, the Roman commander gathered the surviving slaves together and told them that they could avoid a torturous death if they would only identify "the slave called Spartacus." The actor Kirk Douglas, who played the role of Spartacus, was about to step forward when another slave advanced first saying, "I am Spartacus." A moment later, a second did the same, then another, until there was a momentous chorus of voices thundering, "I am Spartacus."

More recently, I attended the inauguration of Dr. Tracy Fitzsimmons, President of Shenandoah University. The featured speaker was Dr. Maya Angelou. She first spoke of the dark clouds that gather in all our lives, but then she imagined a rainbow emerging from them leading to a brighter day. Her message was not only one of hope for those who suffer, but also a call for us to become the rainbows in other people's lives. After the event, I witnessed Dr. Angelou meeting with a select group from her audience. I watched as she held out her arms to a student majoring in voice. I only heard a snippet of their conversation—Dr. Angelou asserting, "The first language you want to learn is Italian." The student was hanging on her every word.

Behaviors based upon rewards and punishments are dependent upon the external stimuli of outside parties. If the rewards or punishments are removed, there is no motivation for behavior. Those who are inspired, however, are intrinsically motivated—they "own" the desired outcome and have a sense of purpose in making it come into being. They more likely have a greater sense of self, a heightened presence and stand taller in their own shoes.

Since even the best systems of rewards and punishments cannot anticipate every circumstance, behaviors thus motivated are often misaligned with what is best for organizations. Organizations that inspire their members have two advantages. First, those inspired look beyond their self-interests to act according to the best interests of the enterprise. Second, motivation based upon an internalized sense of purpose is usually much more powerful than that based upon external stimuli alone. Those organizations whose members embrace a shared sense of purpose will enjoy a competitive advantage over entities that rely solely upon rewards and punishments.

To lead by inspiration is not the same as to lead by charisma. Either servant leaders or self-focused leaders may be charismatic. Followers of those who are servant leaders have a sense of purpose and a heightened sense of self. While followers of self-focused charismatic leaders also have a sense of purpose, their sense of self is diminished. For this latter group, allegiance is not so much to a higher cause, but rather to such leaders themselves—following them wherever they go and doing whatever they command. However, it is not critical that leaders be charismatic to be inspiring. Winston Churchill inspired the British people to fight on in the Battle of Britain. I have never heard anyone describe him as charismatic.

Other than my parents, the most influential person in my youth was my high school football and basketball coach. He had control of the ultimate carrot and stick—whether or not I played in a game. However, it was his strength of character that inspired me. He once kicked three star players off an undefeated basketball team for a rules infraction, and the team then went on to lose the remainder of its games. He was steadfast in doing what he thought was right regardless of the personal consequences to him. His character still inspires me, even though my playing days are long over, and he is now deceased.

Who do you inspire? Who will willingly suffer for a cause you champion? What snippet in your life will be the rainbow that expands someone's horizon? I can imagine a rapt audience in one of the world's great opera houses hanging onto every note of a grown woman singing an aria from Verdi's *La traviata*.

QUESTIONS FOR REFLECTION

- Have you been inspired by anyone in your life? If so, how did this come about?

- How effective are you in using rewards and punishments in influencing others' behaviors? How effective are you in inspiring others?

RELATED CHAPTERS

9

EVERYONE A LEADER

I believe there is a vast reservoir of untapped energy, capacity and wisdom within the people of our typical organizations. A key to unlocking this potential is a shift from the traditional paradigm of *leaders lead* and *followers follow* to a new paradigm—*everyone a leader* and *everyone a follower*.

Many years ago, I toured a woodworking factory that was eventually acquired by American Woodmark. Its plant manager pointed out a worker stacking components coming from a saw. When the manager said the worker had done this same job for over ten years, I quickly formed an impression of his capabilities. That impression was just as quickly shattered when the manager continued by saying that this worker went home after work each day to run a family farm.

The traditional paradigm is that "who leads" and "who follows" is determined by position, status or rank. The word *leader*, however, has as its origin in a Middle English word meaning literally "the one who walks ahead." With this meaning, who leads and who follows is determined not by position or rank, but rather by *behavior*. If we define a leader as "one who acts to influence people to follow a particular direction," then whenever we behave in this way, we become leaders.

If one "walks ahead," it is implied that there is at least one other who follows. A follower is "one who is influenced by another to pursue a particular direction." Whenever we do so, we become followers, regardless of any formal authority we may hold over the person influencing us.

Adopting these definitions leads us to a new paradigm, *everyone a leader* and *everyone a follower*. Some years after my experience in the woodworking factory, a union negotiation at the same facility resulted in workers gaining responsibility for a number of decisions previously made by management. More recently, this organization adopted "lean manufacturing," in which shop-floor workers took a leadership role in determining how to restructure work and improve quality, productivity and safety. These steps helped the organization to transition to this everyone-a-leader, everyone-a-follower perspective.

Organizations can fully adopt this new paradigm by establishing an orientation that all members *approach every situation from the viewpoint that they may lead or follow depending upon the circumstances that unfold*. With this orientation, leaders hold themselves responsible and accountable for acting according to the organization's purpose and values. Even though they may have formal power over others, they see themselves as having a *choice* as to whether and how to share this power. For example, whenever we defer to a technical expert, we are choosing to follow this other person's lead.

Followers also see themselves as having *choices*—whether ot not to follow and in what manner. They are prepared to challenge, question and offer suggestions. They do so without undermining the formal authority of their leaders to lead or relieving themselves of their duty to follow. While they respect the authority of their leaders, they do not blindly fall in step. Rather, they, too, hold themselves accountable to the higher authority of the organization's and their own ethical values.

The *everyone-a-leader* and *everyone-a-follower* orientation has several profound benefits. People don't inherently see others in one-down or one-up positions, and so they are more likely to treat each other with greater dignity and respect. Neither leaders nor followers automatically assume that it is the leader who is "right" or has the "truth." Therefore, both parties will more readily see reality as it is rather than assume that the leader already has the right perspective. Furthermore, followers are more likely to grow, develop their capabilities and become more autonomous. Finally, people will come to work with a sense of ownership of both their individual responsibilities and the organization as a whole. They will be energized, ready to use their talents and willing to share their wisdom. As a result, organizations increase their capacities to be creative, make better decisions, accomplish challenging goals, establish competitive advantages and ultimately behave in a more positive way in keeping with their purposes and values.

Creating the organizational belief that *everyone is a leader* and *everyone is a follower* is a challenging but highly rewarding endeavor. An organization successful in doing so unlocks the vast hidden potential of its members. The impact of this potential, once released, is tremendous.

QUESTIONS FOR REFLECTION

- When you think of the word "leader," what characteristics first come to mind: "position," "rank," "type of behavior" or something else? What about the word "follower?"

- Have you ever been in a formal leadership role where you have acted as a follower as defined here? Similarly, have you been in a follower role and yet acted as a leader? If so, what were the results?

RELATED CHAPTERS

SECTION 2.3

PROCESSES AND TOOLS

This section includes six essays that describe principles and techniques that will aid in the creation and maintenance of exceptional organizations. First, "What Do I Want?" presents a universal process for doing work which is applicable to any situation. Second, "The Much Maligned Meeting" provides a basic format for conducting effective and efficient meetings. Third, "The Survival of the Fittest" shows that effective leaders embrace both competition and cooperation as appropriate techniques depending upon the particular circumstances. Fourth, "'Not Knowing' is Your Friend" describes methods of discourse to better seek the truth of any situation. Fifth, "Yes, Even for Non-Profits" shows the importance of creating a significant and sustainable cash flow for all enterprises. Finally, "Maximizing Profits—Isn't that Our Job?" questions the traditional criteria for decision-making and offers an alternative.

10

"WHAT DO I WANT?"

I believe in the creative orientation, where individuals and organizations seek to create the results they truly desire. This perspective contrasts with the more common perspective where people and organizations respond or react to the events they experience. We do not inherently have one orientation or the other. Rather, we have the potential to shift our perspective toward the creative and thereby be more likely to achieve our aspirations.

As a handout from a seminar on organizational learning, I received a copy of Robert Fritz's, *The Path of Least Resistance*. Fritz, a composer by training, asked how professionals in the arts and sciences created their results. He found that they followed a common creative process that led to their professional success. It did not occur to these creators, however, to apply these same principles to other aspects of their lives. Fritz's insight was to make this process conscious so that anyone could learn to create what they wanted in their lives, both personally and professionally.

Fritz states that as children we learned that circumstances were the predominant forces in our lives. We experienced approval by parents, teachers and other adults for proper responses and disapproval for negative ones. If we were successfully rewarded for our responses, we may have developed a *responsive orientation*, where we adapted well and became good students, employees and citizens in general. If our responses were not rewarded, we may have learned a *reactive orientation* and become cynical, suspicious and rebellious. In either orientation, the driving forces lie in our circumstances. In this view, the forces shaping our lives are external to us. They are out of our control, and as luck would have it, we are powerless to change them.

The creative orientation is quite different. Whereas people in the responsive-reactive orientation organize their lives around the circumstances in them, people in the creative orientation organize them according to what they want to create. The focus of the creative orientation lies in the fundamental question, "What do I want?" or "What are the results I desire to create?" These questions can be asked in any situation without regard to the circumstances that exist. People in this orientation *choose* to pursue what they want and act to bring their creations into being. With this orientation, power is not external to their circumstances, but rather internal within them. Or as George Bernard Shaw said, "You see things as they are and say, 'Why?' But I dream things that never were and say, 'Why not?'"

After reading his book, I modified Fritz's description of the creative process into a format that I thought applicable not only to individuals but also to organizations. I called this format, *The 7-Step Process*:

THE 7-STEP PROCESS

1. Create a vision
2. Understand current reality
3. Take action
4. Measure performance
5. Modify action
6. Achieve results
7. Create a new vision

Fundamental to this process is what Fritz calls *structural tension*, which results from the discrepancy between what we want (step 1) and what we have (step 2). Once the tension between our vision and current reality is established, movement follows the *path of least resistance*. We take action (step 3) to shift reality toward the desired result. We measure our performance (step 4) and modify our actions as necessary (step 5) until we achieve our desired result (step 6). Once we have achieved this result, we create a new vision (step 7).

In *The Path of Least Resistance for Managers*, Fritz differentiated organizations that have *oscillating structures,* where temporary successes are followed by repeated setbacks, from those having *advancing structures*, which experience continuing growth and success over time. In structures that oscillate, leaders react or respond to events, whereas in those that advance, they create structural tension—in this case, between the desired state for the organization and its existing state.

In 1989, American Woodmark created a "1995 Vision" to restructure its strategic direction and to change its culture in support of this new direction. During its transition, the company introduced the 7-Step Process, which eventually became the primary management tool used to run the business. We applied it to situations, large and small, wherever we could ask the question, "What do we want?" After several setbacks, we accomplished our 1995 Vision. With its successful resolution, we initiated and substantially achieved successive six-year visions in 2001, 2007 and 2013. The company is now initiating its 2019 Vision. Over time, American Woodmark has been successful in creating an advancing structure.

By adapting a creative orientation and applying the creative process, organizations are more likely to establish bold visions, better understand reality and work in alignment to achieve goals. As a result, these organizations advance and achieve their desired results. Similarly, their members, rather than respond or react to circumstances, create what they truly desire, both in their professional and personal lives.

QUESTIONS FOR REFLECTION

- Have you ever responded or reacted to events? What would be an example?

- Have you ever created what you wanted to create? What would be an example?

- Do you see yourself as having a more dominant tendency toward the responsive-reactive orientation or to that of the creative?

RELATED CHAPTERS

- Essay: "Any Luck?": 121

- Lessons: The 7-Step Process: 183
  Working in Alignment: 244

11

THE MUCH MALIGNED MEETING

I believe that meetings get a bum rap! The frequent wrath of meeting goers is largely misguided. The reality is that meetings are vital to organizational success—perhaps that's why we conduct so many of them. Whatever frustrations we feel about meetings are better focused upon our lack of skills in conducting them. Fortunately, these skills are readily learnable. When applied, they substantially multiply our personal and organizational effectiveness.

Most leaders have little or no awareness of how to properly conduct a meeting or the consequences of not doing so. Participants are often left wondering, "Why am I here?" "What are we trying to accomplish?" "Why is one person dominating the conversation?" "Why can't we reach a conclusion?" "How could I better use my time if I were not here?" Emotions range from indifference and boredom to anger, cynicism and regret.

For many years, American Woodmark had no established technique for conducting meetings. As a result, quality varied according to the skill of each meeting's leader—none of whom had any formal training in the subject. One year, we engaged a consultant who provided us with a meeting management process. He presented a sixty page manual of how to conduct meetings, which we dutifully followed in pilot programs. It was soon apparent, however, that this technique would not work. It was too complex, and it conflicted with some of our established management principles. Before long, we dismissed him and his process.

After this experience, we concluded that we needed to take a more basic approach and create a methodology that would be applicable to virtually any meeting situation. We established the following format:

STANDARD MEETING FORMAT

- Icebreaker

- Review agenda

- Set expectations

- Content

- Next step

- Review expectations

- Feedback

While each step was critical, three were unusual to traditional meeting management tools: *set expectations, review expectations* and *feedback*. By asking attendees to state their expectations, the participants created a shared vision for what constituted a successful meeting. Expectations that could not be met were noted at the start thus reducing the disappointment of not being addressed later on. Second, by reviewing expectations at the end of the meeting, there was a recognition as to whether or not the participants' expectations were successfully met. Third, by asking leaders and participants to provide feedback—not only on meeting content but also on the way the meeting was conducted—they became observers of their own behavior and over time increased their meeting-management skills. Finally, as par-

ticipants became more comfortable being open in their feedback, they typically developed much greater trust with one
another.

We trained people in this technique across the company,
establishing the rule that all meetings would utilize this format. Collective skill levels increased, and our culture reinforced expectations that the format would be followed. The
implementation was relatively painless. People quickly saw
that their meetings had a purpose, achieved an appropriate
result and did so in a efficient manner. Their effectiveness
further supported their continued use. This tool has stood
the test of time and has since been adopted successfully in
other organizations.

For those institutions suffering from mindless meetings,
using the standard meeting format will likely create quick
and substantial benefits for a relatively limited investment.
For this reason, it can serve as one of the first steps of a
broader cultural-change effort.

QUESTIONS FOR REFLECTION

- Think of an ineffective meeting that you attended.
  What made it ineffective?

- Think of a successful meeting in which you participated. What made it effective?

RELATED CHAPTER

- Lesson: Meeting Management: 196

12

THE SURVIVAL
OF THE FITTEST

I believe in "the survival of the fittest"—not just for life's creatures but also for economic institutions. But what makes such institutions fit? The traditional view is that they know best how to *compete*—how to win by pursuing their own self-interests. I believe, however, that the secret lies not only in understanding how to compete but also in how to *cooperate*—where parties mutually benefit by sharing a concern for one another. The challenge is in knowing when to use one approach over the other.

The case for the traditional view was dramatized by Gordon Gekko in the 1987 film, *Wall Street*. At a shareholders' meeting of Teldar Paper, Gekko, played by Michael Douglas, makes an impassioned plea to convince Teldar shareholders to sell him their company.

The new law of evolution in Corporate America seems to be survival of the un-fittest. But, in my book you either do it right or you get eliminated. The point is, ladies and gentlemen, that greed, for a lack of a better word, greed is good. Greed is good, greed is right, greed works, greed clarifies, cuts through and captures the essence of the evolutionary spirit. Greed in all its forms—greed for life, for money, for love, for knowledge has marked the upward surge of mankind, and greed, you mark my words, will not only save Teldar Paper but that other malfunctioning corporation called the U.S.A.[1]

Gekko's philosophy is supported by two of the most influential authors of all time. In the *Wealth of Nations*, published in 1776, Adam Smith argued that individuals pursuing their own self-interests will not only provide themselves the maximum benefit, but will also create—through "the invisible hand of the marketplace"—the greatest benefit to the overall community. This concept was reinforced in 1859 by Charles Darwin, who in *The Origin of Species*, stated that species are naturally selected to survive based upon their fitness in life's competition. The phrase "survival of the fittest," although not coined by Darwin, came to symbolize his work.

The problem with the traditional view is that it is applied not only to economic institutions that naturally compete for revenues and scarce resources, but to all parties in all situations. The goal is to win—even with employees, suppliers, customers and other stakeholders of the institutions. The assumption is that all parties are in conflict with each pursuing their own respective self-interests.

When I started working for Boise Cascade's cabinet division, the owner of the predecessor company to American Woodmark was my boss. He was a bully. Sitting in his office one day, I witnessed him become incensed when our sales manager came in to express his difficulty in getting a key customer to accept the phase out of a product line critical to that customer's business. At that moment, he picked up the phone, got the customer on the line and said in an angry voice, "Sam, this is Al. We are phasing out the Windsor line." Without waiting for a reply, he slammed down the phone, turned to our sales manager and said, "There, it's done." Because he had many talents, the business was financially successful, but for only as long as he could directly control it. He sold the business to Boise for a substantial sum, but continued to run it. As the business grew, however, he lost his ability to maintain control. He eventually left Boise, leaving the business in a chaotic state. Clearly, this organization was not "fit for survival."

Most people are unaware that Adam Smith wrote a second book, the *Theory of Moral Sentiments*, which opens with the following sentence:

> *How selfish soever man may be supposed, there are evidently some principles in his nature, which interest him in the fortunes of others, and render their happiness necessary to him, though he derives nothing from it except the pleasure of seeing it.*[2]

Smith stated that part of being a moral person was having a concern for others, as well as for oneself. As described in David Loye's book, *Darwin's Lost Theory*, Charles Darwin also wrote a second book, *The Descent of Man*, in which Darwin postulated that a key part of humankind's successful evolution was our ability to cooperate with one another. Based upon their writings, neither Smith nor Darwin would endorse a philosophy of "greed is good."

As part of a cultural-change initiative at American Woodmark, we strove to interact with all stakeholders on the basis of *cooperation first and conflict second*. This approach was initially disorienting to union representatives, with whom we had historically acted as hard-nosed adversaries, and to our suppliers and customers, whom we had treated on a win/lose basis—negotiating a price paid for the services rendered. We engaged the union to give workers greater responsibility on the shop floor for decisions previously made by management. We also initiated formal partnership programs with vendors and customers to better understand the details of each others' businesses to find opportunities for mutual gain. While the elements of competing self-interests were still very much present—particularly with product pricing with customers

and vendors, and wage-scale negotiations with the union—
they became of lesser importance to overall relationships.

It would be naïve to assume that some level of cooperation is always possible. In *People of the Lie*, Scott Peck indicated that some individuals are so self-focused, and in some
cases genuinely evil, that the only way to relate to them is on
the basis of *power*. For example, at American Woodmark, we
once were ending a relationship with a major customer who
owed us a considerable sum and whom we feared would stop
paying us once his phase-out needs were met. We refused
to send him any more product until his account was paid in
full, and we made subsequent shipments on a cash-before-
delivery basis.

While competition and self-interest are necessary for survival, to be sustainable an enterprise also needs to embrace
the principles of cooperation, concern for others and partnership—knowing when to use one orientation over the other.
It is important to remember that by the end of the movie
Gordon Gekko's world had collapsed.

QUESTIONS FOR REFLECTION

- Do you see your organization's relationships with
  various stakeholders—clients, suppliers, employees,
  shareholders and the communities in which you operate—based more upon competition or cooperation?

- Under what circumstances does your organization
  benefit from a competitive orientation? When is a co-
  operative orientation more advantageous?

RELATED CHAPTERS

- Essay: Yes, Even in Business: 52

- Lesson: Culture: 150

13

"*NOT KNOWING*
IS YOUR FRIEND"

I believe that *debate*—where the focus is upon winning an argument rather than seeking the truth—is overused and overvalued within organizations and society in general. On the contrary, other forms of discourse—when used to understand the truth and seek a better result—are mostly misunderstood and largely neglected.

In 1991, I attentively watched the television coverage of the Senate Judiciary Committee confirmation hearings on the nomination of Clarence Thomas to the Supreme Court. Of particular interest was the testimony of Anita Hill, who had worked for Thomas. When asked in an FBI background interview, she described Thomas' behaviors, which, if true, could be construed as sexual harassment. In my naïveté—it was the first time that I had actually watched a congressional hearing—I had assumed that all members of the Committee, both Republicans and Democrats, would want to learn the truth—whether or not Thomas had in fact behaved this way. Actually, *none* of the Committee members gave this impression. When Hill testified, most members spent the majority of their allotted time speaking to the cameras rather than asking her questions. When they spoke, those favoring the nomination framed their comments and questions in a manner that disparaged Hill, while those against the nomination framed theirs in her support. There were other women available who might have shed greater light on this matter, but they were never allowed to testify. The Senate narrowly confirmed Thomas' nomination, and I lost one pair of my rose-colored glasses.

In retrospect, the Clarence Thomas hearings simply mirrored how people in America typically relate to one another. Most people value having their positions affirmed—regardless of their validity—over finding the truth of the matter. This preference is reinforced by our legal system, where the prosecution and the defense each argue the case from their respective sides. They are not expected to seek the truth, but rather to win the case. While this may be the best way to run a legal system, an over emphasis on asserting one's position or winning a debate can be devastating for organizations.

Shortly after the Clarence Thomas hearings, I read Peter M. Senge's, already cited, *The Fifth Discipline*. It not only put my frustrations with the hearings into perspective, but also provided a framework for understanding two types of discourse—*discussion* and *dialogue*.

The purpose of discussion is to "present and defend different views." Participants advocate their positions, evaluate alternative thoughts and reduce these alternatives until a common position is established. Discussion falls into two categories. The first is "debate," where the intent is to win one's position rather than to seek the truth. The parties often view *opinions* as *facts* and believe that their opinions are "the truth." Since they "know the truth," they neither seek input nor consider evidence to the contrary.

The second category of discussion is "truth seeking" where the intent is to find the truth, best conclusion or course of action. Here participants hold their opinions or *mental models*—that is, their internal pictures of the world—up to scrutiny to better understand reality and make better choices. They consider their initial positions as opinions to be questioned, not facts to be asserted. Since they don't know the truth, they seek it.

The purpose of dialogue is to "present different perspectives as a means to discovering a new perspective not anticipated by any one party." Where discussion incorporates elements of advocacy and competition—that is, one idea in opposition to another—dialogue encompasses cooperation, group learning and idea creation. Dialogue is particularly useful when the subject matter is complex. By its very nature, dialogue is an attempt to seek the truth.

Organizations spend the vast majority of their time interacting in debate rather than truth-seeking discussion or dialogue. Think of organizations that have either suffered mightily or failed altogether because they held mental models of their environment significantly at variance with reality. An example is the internet industry in the late 1990s. Internet start-up companies assumed that a new economic reality would support ever increasing stock prices and that they could continually sell shares to the public. When this belief proved false and the market crashed, most of these start-ups went bankrupt.

While there are tools to better learn how to effectively use discussion and dialogue, the fundamental choice is one of intent. Do you "know the truth," or do you seek it? Is winning more important than knowing, or knowing more important than winning? While debate may be appropriate in some instances, a basic orientation of "seeking the truth"—not knowing it—is a critical advantage for organizations and their members. "Not knowing" is your friend.

QUESTIONS FOR REFLECTION

- Think of a time when you were part of a group seeking to make a decision. In what type of discourse did the other participants engage? In what type did you engage?

● Recall an instance where you tried to "win an argument." How open were you to learning new information, changing your opinions and siding with the
other party?

RELATED CHAPTER

● Lesson: Mental Models: 210

14

YES, EVEN FOR NON-PROFITS

I believe in profits—yes, even for non-profits. The reality is that to be sustainable, all organizations must generate revenues equal to or greater than what they spend. The mechanism that creates this relationship is the *business strategy*—an integral element of the *vision-driven* organization.

A business strategy, also referred to as a *business model*, is the vehicle by which organizations generate profits—or, as some non-profits prefer to say, "excess revenues over expenses." By so doing, for-profit organizations create wealth for owners, while non-profits generate cash reserves—the equivalent of wealth—to be held by them for the public good. A viable business strategy creates a sustainable competitive advantage, meaning that customers, clients and benefactors value their products, services or causes more than they do the offerings of competing organizations. Such strategies are critical if institutions are to achieve their missions.

I first met Dr. James Davis, former President of Shenandoah University, in 1984 when he came to my office and asked me to get involved with the institution. Not long after, I joined its Board of Trustees. Davis came to Shenandoah in 1982 in a time of crisis. The institution had low enrollments, high-fixed costs, excess capacity, few cash reserves, virtually no endowment and a small alumni base. To survive, salaries were frozen, staff was cut and extraordinary efforts were made to meet payrolls. At the time, Shenandoah did not have a viable business strategy, but dearly needed one.

Under Davis' leadership, a new direction evolved. Since the potential for further expense reductions was limited, the only opportunity was a strategy for greater revenue growth. Shenandoah created a two-pronged business model, which—in addition to addressing the school's immediate needs—served the institution well for the next twenty years. The first was a focus on gaining financial support from members of its local communities. Critical to this was the creation among donors of a sense of ownership in the success of the institution, even though most were not alumni. The second was the development of new academic programs which were not only self-funding through tuitions and fees but also generated contributions to overhead benefiting the institution overall. The focus of this initiative was the creation of highly sought graduate programs which were in demand nationally. These had the advantage of not requiring the significant financial-aid support required of undergraduate programs. Over Davis' twenty-six year tenure, Shenandoah increased the quality of instruction, established graduate programs in eight key areas, expanded enrollment from 900 to 3000 and became a regional university with several nationally recognized programs. While not the only factor, none of this would have been possible without a viable business strategy. Under the leadership of Dr. Tracy Fitzsimmons, who succeeded Davis as Shenandoah's president in 2008, the institution continues to prosper and grow—with a new strategy built upon the successes of the past.

Many institutions develop five-year or ten-year plans that are little more than extrapolations of past trends into the future. Annual budgeting becomes an exercise where those at lower levels vie for a greater percentage of the organization's resources, and senior management decides how best to split the pie. Frequently, leaders of successful enterprises are not even aware of their entities' underlying business strategies. Often such leaders took the helm when times were good and implicitly assumed that they would remain so. It usually takes a crisis for such individuals to examine their business strategies—and often too late. With the most recent economic downturn, many leaders found that what had worked for decades had become obsolete.

Early in my career, I had the fortune of leading American Woodmark's predecessor company through an economic downturn. I have subsequently led American Woodmark through two others. Each instance made us acutely aware of the strengths and weaknesses of our business model and afforded us the freedom to make difficult choices that might not have been available in better times. In each situation, our vision was not only to survive the downturn but also to enhance our competitive posture as we exited it. None of these initiatives were made as part of the normal budgeting and business planning cycle.

For either a for-profit or non-profit institution, there is no alternative but to create a viable business strategy where the organization sustains a competitive advantage and a positive cash flow. While not the only factor, viable business strategies are crucial to the creation of exceptional organizations.

QUESTIONS FOR REFLECTION

- Can you articulate the business strategy for any for-profit or non-profit organization for which you are or were a member?

- Have you been a member of an organization that went through a severe change in its environment? If so, did its business strategy change? How did this come about?

RELATED CHAPTER

- Lesson: Vision-Driven Organizations: 130

15

"MAXIMIZING PROFITS— ISN'T THAT OUR JOB?"

The common belief is that the goal of for-profit business organizations is to maximize profits and by implication shareholder value. What seems to have gone unnoticed is the fact that it is actually impossible to make decisions using this standard as a criterion. Also unnoticed is the perverse consequences of attempting to do so. Could the conventional wisdom be wrong?

At some point in history, an economist came up with the proposition that people are "rational," and that by being rational, business leaders will make decisions based upon maximizing profits in any particular situation. Over the years, this view has become ingrained as a fundamental principle of most economic theory and is now immortalized in virtually every introductory economics textbook.

Profit maximization became thought of as a benefit to society, as evidenced by the *American Law Institute's Principles of Corporate Governance* which states:

> *... a corporation ... should have as its objective the conduct of business activities with a view to enhance profits and shareholder gain.*[1]

So the enhancement of shareholder value is not only a good thing, it is a legal principle.

Citigroup's business leaders have given every appearance of attempting to maximize profits. Over the years, Citigroup grew to become a huge diversified financial services giant revered by the business press. In the late 1990s, it successfully championed the lobbying efforts that resulted in Congress reducing regulatory restraints on banks. Unfortunately, there is a slight blemish on its otherwise stellar record. In the most recent economic crisis, Citigroup was so overexposed to the mortgage market that to survive it required a massive bailout from the Federal Reserve which gave the United States 36 percent of its equity and control of its destiny.

Citigroup's experience exposes some of the fallacies of the profit-maximization principle. Since profit maximization implies that all behaviors should be focused on this result to the exclusion of others, it follows that the enterprise should be willing to accept whatever risk is required to achieve this outcome. In Citigroup's case, this orientation led to an overexposure to potentially profitable, yet in retrospect, highly risky loans and investments. It also implies that Citigroup's stakeholders other than shareholders don't matter—its depositors, bondholders, employees and the world financial system.

What profit maximization does imply is the maximization of shareholder value. But who are the shareholders? For public corporations, are they—individuals who have owned the company's stock since its inception, traders who may own the stock for less than a day, or potential investors being courted to buy stock for the future? Second, what is the time frame over which profits are maximized,—a day, a month, a quarter, a year or longer? Finally, what is the measurement of profits—after-tax earnings, earnings per share, return on invested capital, the net present value of discounted cash flows or an increase in share price? Since there is considerable ambiguity as to what we mean by profit maximization, it is impossible to have one criterion upon which to make choices.

The reality is that no organization actually does make decisions based solely upon profit maximization. The level of risk is questioned, other stakeholders are considered and a range of criteria are addressed to meet various stakeholder interests. However, a strong bias toward the perceived principle of profit maximization may lead boards of directors to seeing their role as primarily representing shareholders. As a result, they tend to create incentive systems for managers based almost exclusively upon financial performance, frequently rewarding greater levels of risk-taking and shorter rather than a longer time frames. Probably the greatest fallacy of a profit-maximization belief is that it keeps business leaders from focusing upon what is really important.

Business organizations are conceived by their founders to achieve purposes that typically go far beyond simply making a profit. Where this is the case, shareholders are enlisted as a means to achieve these purposes, realizing that these shareholders expect a return on their investments for doing so. In a similar manner, other stakeholders are enlisted— employees, customers, suppliers, communities, even society in general—all of which expect value for their contributions.[2]

I believe that leaders should make decisions based upon *the best interests of the enterprise as a whole*, which includes pursuing its mission, maintaining its long-term viability and providing value to all stakeholders. Acting this way does not require that the needs of every stakeholder be well met all of the time. This would be impossible to do. On the contrary, depending upon the circumstances, some stakeholder needs must be subordinated to others. For example, in a severe economic downturn dividends may be cut to conserve cash to fund customer promotions. These actions, while serving the organization as a whole, would in the short run benefit customers to the detriment of shareholders. Alternatively, temporary pay cuts would benefit shareholders at the expense of employees. There is no formula for determining what is in the best interests of the organization. Leaders must weigh all of the variables and use their best judgment to reach their decisions.

Profits for shareholders, just like the returns to all stakeholders, are a residual result of running the enterprise effectively and efficiently. The irony is that by acting in the best interests of the organization overall, the enterprise is more likely to thrive, with all stakeholders benefiting in a superior way over time.

Like all public companies, American Woodmark's share price is advantaged if its reported earnings per share are slightly above its prior year's earning's level rather than slightly below. Kent Guichard, when he was our chief financial officer, closed our books one quarter and later told me that we had earned one cent less than the prior year. I recall saying that it was a shame that we did not earn just two cents more so that we could report a slight gain. He told me that there was enough discretion in the various accrual and reserve accounts to have done so, but that our results were based upon previously agreed to estimates of these account valuations made by his staff. He thought it important that our finance team know that it was their job to prepare an accurate presentation of our financial results, not to arbitrarily change reserve levels after the fact in order to make our earnings appear better. While Kent's behavior did not "maximize" profits or shareholder value in the moment, it did send a message to his team, to the organization as a whole and even to the investment community that actions to artificially improve results in the short term at the expense of the long term were unacceptable, not consistent with the company's values and not in the best long-term interest of the organization.

It is not the job of business leaders to maximize shareholder value, nor to maximize the value received by any other stakeholder. All parties are responsible for acting in their own best interests. In the case of public corporations, shareholders can buy shares, sell shares already owned, or vote to add or replace directors. These potential actions can be evaluated relative to other alternatives in the pursuit of their desired investment returns.

The *American Law Institute's Principles of Corporate Governance* also states that in the event of an unsolicited tender offer to acquire a company that there are:

> ... *circumstances in which the board may give weight to groups or interests separate from the shareholders that may be negatively affected by a tender offer that could be said to favor the interests of shareholders. ... Such groups and interests would include, for example, environmental or other community concerns, and may include groups such as employees, suppliers and customers.*[3]

Even our legal system has concluded that it is okay for business leaders to consider stakeholders other than shareholders alone in its deliberations.

By acting in the organization's best interests rather than attempting to maximize profits, the enterprise is much more likely to create extraordinary shareholder value over the long term. Not only will the enterprise thrive, but so will all of its stakeholders.

QUESTIONS FOR REFLECTION

- For organizations where you have worked, what did its leaders see as their primary responsibility? What criteria were used to measure performance relative to this criterion? How did these measures influence decisions?

- Have you been in a situation where acting in accordance with established performance targets was inconsistent with what you thought would be in the best interests of the enterprise? How did you resolve this dilemma?

RELATED CHAPTER

- Essay: Yes, Even in Business: 52

SECTION 2.4

THE JOURNEY

This section presents six essays that describe the nature of journeys taken to create exceptional organizations. It highlights the commitment, the willingness to be wrong, the flexibility to change and the perseverance required of leaders who undertake such ventures. First, "Talk is Cheap" showcases the difference between adopting a statement of values on paper and acting according to them in reality. Second, "Guidance from Gandhi" offers insights into overcoming barriers to cultural change. Third, "A Bad Plan Poorly Executed" shows how easy it is to get off-track by following what is considered "best practices"—in this instance, the delegation of decision-making authority when working in teams. Fourth, "Right Person / Right Job" acknowledges the universal desire to fill every position with a highly effective individual with the challenge of building a structure to do so. Fifth, "Why Do Exceptional Organizations Fail?" shows that once established, exceptional organizations must be vigilant to maintain their status. Finally, "Any Luck?" makes the somewhat contradictory point that while we cannot control events, we can choose to make a difference in our own lives and the lives of others.

16

TALK IS CHEAP

Talk is cheap! While virtually all organizations of any size embrace statements of values to guide ethical behavior, few actually live up to them. Unfortunately, creating an organization whose values are embraced in reality, rather than just on paper, is a daunting task.

In July 2000, a multi-billion dollar corporation issued a sixty-four page Code of Ethics, which included, along with its vision to be the world leader in its industry, the following values' statement:

OUR VALUES

RESPECT: We treat others as we would like to be treated ourselves. We do not tolerate abusive or disrespectful treatment. Ruthlessness, callousness and arrogance do not belong here.

INTEGRITY: We work with customers and prospects openly, honestly and sincerely. When we say we will do something, we will do it; when we say we cannot or will not do something, then we won't do it.

COMMUNICATION: We have an obligation to communicate. Here we take the time to talk with one another...and to listen. We believe that information is meant to move and that information moves people.

EXCELLENCE: We are satisfied with nothing less than the very best in everything we do. We will continue to raise the bar for everyone. The great fun here will be for all of us to discover just how good we really can be.[1]

In December 2001, this same enterprise filed for bankruptcy, and shortly thereafter its chairman, president and other senior officers were convicted of fraud and other crimes. The Smithsonian Institution secured a copy of the corporation's Code of Ethics for its archives. This company was Enron.

Some organizations' leaders have no interest in living up to their stated values. Their goal is to deceive stakeholders into believing that they are more virtuous than they truly are. Others, however, genuinely want their organizations to act according to espoused values, but for whatever reason, are unable to do so.

Some years ago, American Woodmark created a mission statement to describe the company's purpose, values and expected behaviors. Our values were organized around four guiding principles: *customer satisfaction, integrity, teamwork* and *excellence*. The initial response from employees after its introduction was overwhelmingly positive, and we waited in anticipation for behaviors to change. The first tangible reaction, however, was one of confusion and frustration. The reality was that our company provided good but not great customer satisfaction, acted with integrity some but not all of the time, did not work in teams and was far from excellent. Employees attempting to act according to the guidelines were soon confronted by difficult-to-resolve barriers preventing them from doing so. For example, when we manufactured a product with less than desired quality, our quality-control personnel began holding up shipments. However, our machinery was incapable of consistently producing a product up to standard, and we were therefore confronted with the choice of shipping substandard product or nothing at all. We shipped the substandard product, and our employees soon learned to ignore the mission statement. Their behaviors reverted back to where they had been before.

It was not until three years later when as part of a broader initiative, our 1995 Vision, we made a committed effort to live up to the principles of our mission statement. We created enhanced quality and service processes, established procedures for working in teams, taught employees how to resolve ethical dilemmas and, in general, enhanced management effectiveness. It took six years for our behaviors to reach a minimum degree of alignment with our mission statement values.

Merely telling people that they must behave differently just doesn't work. To make such changes require the creation of specific processes and structures that enable the organization to act according to its desired standards. Depending upon the circumstances, creating value-based entities may take days, months or years. In the interim, it is important to present one's value statement as an aspiration to be pursued rather than as a reality already achieved.

Value-based organizations have long-term competitive advantages. If given the choice, most people would prefer working in such institutions, and clients, suppliers and other stakeholders would likewise prefer relationships with such enterprises over those more typically available. Talk is cheap—but creating a value-based organization in reality, not just on paper, is something to treasure.

QUESTIONS FOR REFLECTION

- Have you been a member of an organization that had a statement of values? How well did the organization and its members live up to them?

- Have you been in a situation where it seemed impossible for you to live up the organization's stated values? How did you resolve this situation?

RELATED CHAPTERS

17

GUIDANCE FROM GANDHI

Organizational cultures are naturally resistant to change. But what if we want to change them? While I believe that we can do so successfully, the path is not obvious. There are unanticipated twists and turns, and the terrain is covered with sticks and stones.

We can define the *culture* of an organization as the *beliefs, values, traditions* and *processes* that determine its behavior. A culture is a *system* because its elements function together as a whole, and it is a *stable* system in that its behaviors tend to remain constant even when the outside environment changes. To create a new culture requires not only positive actions to move toward the desired state, but also steps to remove barriers that keep the existing culture in place.

As mentioned in the case study, American Woodmark introduced, as part of its 1995 Vision, a standardized management process for creating results. We asked the senior management team at all locations to learn to use these techniques and then to train those lower in their organizations to do the same. During a visit to one such location, I asked the senior team how they liked the new initiative. They said that they found it very beneficial for lower-level management. I then asked about their own experience using the process, at which point the location manager responded, "Our senior team doesn't need the new tools, our existing techniques work just fine." So much for embracing change!

As a result of this visit, our corporate leadership team suspended the rollout of the program to reassess how best to proceed. We concluded that we would start the training over again and would require proficiency in the use of the process at each organizational level before taking the training to the next lower level. We began by reestablishing our own use of these techniques. This approach eventually proved successful. However, what was thought to be a six-month implementation took three years for completion with further fits and starts along the way. While initially everyone was excited about the new program's potential—"to take us toward a desired state," we had not anticipated the resistance to giving up established habits and work patterns—"the barriers that keep existing behaviors in place."

Everyone believes in change, provided it happens to someone else. Few of us are willing to change our own behavior, and the higher we are in the organization's hierarchy the less willing we are to do so. After all, we arrived at our current positions precisely because we already knew what to do.

When as leaders we are tempted to create a new organizational culture, we must remember that our own behavior is part of the existing culture. So where do we begin? I believe that we can take our guidance from Gandhi who said that if you want to change the world, you must start by changing yourself. This is not an easy task. We must not only overcome established routines, but also the negative feedback from the existing culture that will fight to keep us in our place. As we persevere, we will find that this culture will begin to shift in a positive direction in part because we, as an element of the system, have shifted our own behavior.

Cultural change is a difficult, chaotic undertaking. Furthermore, it requires that we move out of our personal comfort zones and embrace new behaviors. The decision to pursue such an initiative should not be taken lightly. However, when successful, it can be transformational for both the individual and the organization.

QUESTIONS FOR REFLECTION

- Have you ever been part of a cultural-change effort? If so, what were the anticipated benefits? Were there any barriers to change? How did the initiative go?

- Have you ever led a cultural-change effort either for an enterprise as a whole or for a team or department within it? If so, did you undergo any personal transformations yourself as part of the process? If so, how did this come about?

RELATED CHAPTERS

18

A BAD PLAN POORLY EXECUTED

I once believed in employee *empowerment*, defined as "individuals and teams acting with ownership, freedom and accountability while fulfilling job responsibilities." I also believed in making decisions by *consensus*, where teams "collectively come to an agreement that all team members can accept." Why would I not believe in them? They were highly touted by the leading management gurus of the day.

As part of our 1995 Vision, we looked for an overall theme that would characterize American Wooodmark's desire to have all employees be more responsible, take greater initiative, be more productive and embrace a sense of ownership in their jobs. We came up with the theme, "Employee Empowerment—How We Run the Company." With the help of a consultant, we developed various training tools to instruct employees on how they could put this principle into practice.

We organized work into two categories; first, that which could be done by *natural-work teams* comprised of people who work together on a daily basis; and second, that which necessitated *cross-functional teams*, composed of people pulled together from different departments to accomplish a specific task. The teams were instructed to make significant decisions by consensus.

We launched these initiatives with much fanfare and great anticipation. While we had some initial success, we soon realized we had created a monster. The natural-work teams were *empowered* to create "Daily Improvement Plans"—whereby they initiated actions to make improvements in their work areas. This effort was successful so long as the improvements were within their control. Unfortunately, most required assistance from others in the organization, who soon became flooded with requests for assistance. Before long, everyone became disillusioned as requests were delayed or not filled. Furthermore, department managers of natural-work team members were confused about their authority. All teams reported to managers higher in the organization, but the managers were not officially included in the teams. Could they "tell" their teams to take a particular stand on a specific issue? If they could, the team's ability to reach a consensus would be disempowered. If they could not, then their authority over their own direct reports would be compromised. In our effort to *empower* our people, we had undermined the traditional decision-making structure and leadership authority of the company.

At the same time, cross-functional teams were commissioned to achieve tasks that cut across the organization. While many proposed solutions were satisfactory, others were frequently vetoed by those higher up in the hierarchy to the great consternation of those on the team who had assumed that their "consensus decisions" were a company commitment.

Shortly after we embarked on this team effort, our senior leadership team learned of the work of Tannenbaum and Schmidt, who in 1958 wrote a *Harvard Business Review* article titled, "How to Choose a Leadership Pattern." Tannenbaum and Schmidt argued that there was no one ideal pattern for decision-making for a leader, but rather a range of possible styles depending upon the circumstances. At one extreme, the leader may appropriately choose a very directive style and announce a decision, "There is a fire in the dust collection system! Turn off the power!" At the other extreme, the leader might give subordinates the freedom to make their own choices within limits, "Your team can decide who works next week, as long as all functions are covered." What is important is that leaders choose the right style for the right circumstance. When they do, subordinates willingly support the leaders' decisions and experience a sense of ownership, responsibility and accountability. We concluded that the work of Tannenbaum and Schmidt made sense, and we adopted their approach.

Upon reflection, our focus on *empowerment* and *consensus*, was based upon a faulty assumption. We had believed that giving people freedom of choice was inherently better than being directive. We assumed that our traditional leadership structure led naturally to more directive decision-making and that directive decision-making was inherently a bad thing. Therefore, we concluded that we had to create new structures that would compensate for the ones already in place.

With our new perspective, we reorganized our natural-work teams according to the traditional management hierarchy. All supervisors became team leaders, and their direct reports became team members. As with a traditional management hierarchy, the team leaders retained full leadership responsibility and authority. Cross-functional team leaders were given leadership authority within boundaries set by senior management. All supervisors were trained in the principles advocated by Tannenbaum and Schmidt. Finally, we eliminated the guideline of making decisions by consensus.

I believe that people want to be part of a team led by leaders who use the right decision-making patterns for the circumstances. When this is the case, they will be responsible, accountable and have a sense of ownership in the desired result. The words "empowerment" and "consensus" are no longer in my vocabulary.

QUESTIONS FOR REFLECTION

- Were you ever part of a team responsible for making a proposed recommendation or for completing a specific task? If so, how were decisions made? How effective was this process?

- What is your decision-making style? Do you tend to have one pattern regardless of the circumstances or does your style vary?

RELATED CHAPTERS

19

RIGHT PERSON / RIGHT JOB

Nearly everyone who has ever led an organization believes in having the *right person* in the *right job*. The challenge, of course, is to create an environment where this result can actually take place.

A number of years ago, Jake Gosa, who would later succeed me as CEO of American Woodmark, and I went on one of many mini-retreats where we would periodically attempt to solve issues facing the company. On this particular occasion, we wrestled with how best to express our vision of the human resource requirements of the organization. In our deliberations, we came up with the phrase "right person / right job." It captured our thinking. We thought that if our leadership team at each level of the organization would use this simple phrase as a standard for organizing work and placing people in particular jobs, we would create a superior human resource capacity aligned with the company's needs. Quite pleased with our creation, we returned from the retreat, got buy-in from the rest of our senior leadership team and proceeded to introduce this concept.

As we rolled it out, everyone appeared to accept the principle. One day, however, I presented it to the leadership team of one of our manufacturing plants. That evening over dinner with the team, the plant manager expressed a concern, shared among his staff, that they saw themselves as "regular" or "average" people and that they did not know if they met the category of being the "right persons" for their own jobs. At that moment, I did not know either, nor could I reference any specific criteria used by the company to answer this question. Although the company had at the time what I considered to be a standard performance evaluation process, it was a highly subjective one based upon each supervisor's prerogatives. With our "right person / right job" principle, we were attempting to raise our standards, but it soon became clear that using these simple words did nothing but frustrate those who we expected to implement this change. After this interchange at dinner, I returned to the corporate office. Our senior leadership team soon agreed that we would remove the phrase "right person / right job" from the company's lexicon.

The reality is that, while the concept of an organization having the right people in the right jobs is easy to embrace, creating an environment where this condition can actually exist is a different matter. It requires a number of interrelated human resource procedures. These include recruitment, performance evaluation, compensation, training and personal growth and development. I do not believe the creation of these systems can be delegated to outside consultants or traditional staff departments, but rather must be conceived by the organization's senior leadership team tasked with the overall responsibility for running the organization. Since the time that Jake and I held our mini-retreat, it took another ten years for American Woodmark to create the necessary human resource structures to adequately support the "right person / right job" principle.

In addition to the right human resource structures, exceptional organizations require senior leaders who not only have the requisite job skills but also the right values, the fit with the organization's culture and a sense of serving a cause greater than their own self-interests. Ideally these people are promoted from within. Over the last fifteen years of my tenure, serving as either President or Chairman of American Woodmark, we promoted from within whenever feasible. For positions reporting either to the CEO or the chief operating officer, we still needed to hire a number of people from outside the company. Although I thought we did a very thorough job vetting candidates—using a highly regarded search firm, numerous interviews, the feedback of a very competent managerial psychologist and extensive reference checks, only 50 percent of the individuals proved effective in their new positions. Although I was frustrated by our success rate at the time, in retrospect, I believe we had a pretty good batting average. Furthermore, of those that did make the cut, two eventually became exceptional CEOs.

Creating the human resource systems necessary to have the right person in the right job is an arduous, time-consuming task with a long payback period. For these reasons, the effort will likely be preempted from time to time to address more immediate priorities. If created, however, this result will become a major source of long-term competitive advantage.

QUESTIONS FOR REFLECTION

- Have the organizations in which you were a member had the right people in the right jobs? What criteria did you use to reach your conclusion?

- Have you considered yourself the "right person in the right job" for organizations where you have worked? What criteria helped you reach this conclusion?

RELATED CHAPTERS

20

"WHY DO EXCEPTIONAL ORGANIZATIONS FAIL?"

Since a primary characteristic of exceptional organizations is that they are not only viable and valued, but also sustainable, then it should follow that they continue indefinitely. Unfortunately, this is not the case. In reality, some do fail.

The now conventional wisdom is that organizations fail because of external disruptions—changing technology, unanticipated competitive thrusts, altered market dynamics or economic crises. In his insightful book, *The Innovator's Dilemma,* Clayton Christensen explained how difficult it is for organizations that have successful product or service offerings to adopt the next generation of innovations that would at some point supplant what works best for them today. He concluded that success today breeds the seeds of destruction tomorrow.

I believe that Christensen's observations are applicable to all organizations, whether exceptional or not. Exceptional organizations, however, are more likely to survive these disruptions. They typically have financial reserves that give them time and resources to make adjustments. They have inspired competent people who are continually scanning the market and technological landscape ready to make adaptations and reinvent—or disrupt—themselves as required, and they have strong cultures that are a major source of competitive advantage. This does not mean that such entities don't go through turbulent times, but rather they have the resiliency to get through them and usually emerge all the stronger. So, while disruptive technologies may be the demise of some exceptional organizations, I do not believe they are the primary cause.

As a child, I remember going with my mother to a corner poultry shop in the Italian section of downtown Hartford, Connecticut. The shop offered live chickens which were butchered to order on the spot. Eventually, this section of town was targeted for high-rise building development, and all the area shops and restaurants were bought up—all except one. The poultry shop's owner, the butcher, refused to sell. For years, he fought the combined will of the city, its health department, and the legal and financial might of a multi-billion dollar insurance company which wanted his property to complete a city block for a new high rise. Eventually, it was the insurance company that caved, constructing its building on the block, but circumventing the poultry shop, so that the building looked like it had a chipped tooth. Although dwarfed by its surroundings, the poultry shop continued in business. It remained, viable, sustainable and valued—at least to its owner, now providing fresh chickens to office workers on their way home. Many years later on a visit to Hartford, I looked expectantly for the shop, but it was gone.

A person I admired served as the CEO of a public company that I considered to be exceptional based upon its top-of-class industry rankings, superior financial performance and inspired culture. But the company was controlled by a 49 percent owner that wanted to take the company in a new direction for reasons having more to do with its own unique situation than anything else. After an unsuccessful attempt to buy the company, this person retired, several of his senior staff left the organization to become leaders of other entities, and new leadership was brought in from outside. In a small fraction of the time it took to create it, the company's exceptional status was gone.

The poultry shop remained in business for decades, rebuffing every external threat. It presumably did not, however, survive the retirement or death of its owner. Similarly, the public company mentioned above stood at the head of its industry but could not withstand a shift in owner priorities and a consequent leadership change. It is at their peaks that exceptional enterprises are most vulnerable.

It is critical that in the transfer of leadership from one generation to another that new leaders be champions of their entities' aspirations, values and cultures. The ideal place to find such servant leaders is from within the organization's own ranks because such individuals will most likely embrace their entity's unique characteristics. This conclusion is supported by the research of Jim Collins' previously mentioned book, *Good to Great*, who found that of the eleven companies in his study that had gone from *good* to *great*, ten had new CEOs who came from within. This was *six* times the rate of comparison companies, which had not achieved this status.[1]

We have had two CEOs at American Woodmark—Jake Gosa and Kent Guichard—since my retirement. Both were promoted from within and, prior to assuming their roles, had helped shape our organization's culture. Both have been extremely effective.

Ultimately, it is the owners, or their proxies—their directors and trustees—who determine whether or not their organizations remain exceptional, because it is they who determine who leads. One area in which non-profit organizations have an advantage over for-profit entities in remaining exceptional is that their ownership structures do not typically change from one generation to another. Non-profits are held as a public trust. On a trip to England, I visited The University of Oxford, which traces its existence back over eight hundred years. Its ownership has not changed. Owners of for-profit organizations, however, have personal wealth associated with their ownership, which may be sold to meet individual needs or to be distributed to others. The resulting new owners may or may not have an understanding of what characterizes an exceptional organization, much less have a desire to see it continue. How many for-profit organizations, whether exceptional or not, have existed for over one hundred years?

Yes, exceptional organizations do fail. For those leaders who wish to perpetuate such entities, the easier task is dealing with the vagaries of the marketplace. The more serious challenge is determining who will succeed them, and in the case of for-profit entities, influencing owners and their boards of directors to see their institutions as having intrinsic value in their own right, not just as a source of financial wealth.

QUESTIONS FOR REFLECTION

- Whether or not you have worked there, what organizations do you think are exceptional? What is the basis for drawing your conclusions? Are these for-profit or non-profit entities?

- If you have ever worked for an organization you thought was exceptional, do you still consider it so today? What factors have resulted in its either remaining exceptional or failing to do so?

RELATED CHAPTERS

- Essays: To Be Exceptional: 60
            The Servant as Leader: 65

21

"ANY LUCK?"

I believe in luck—both good and bad. Luck is another way of saying that we cannot control events—that we cannot control all of the factors that impact a specific result. However, we can make a difference. Although the idea that "we cannot control events," but that "we can make a difference" may at first appear contradictory, it is not. It is derived from the same concept which has evolved in the scientific community over the past fifty years—namely, that to a much greater degree than ever thought before, all things in our world are interconnected.

In 1960, Edward Lorenz, an MIT meteorologist, used one of the first high-speed main-frame computers to simulate weather patterns. What he found, to his great surprise, was that very small changes in the initial conditions—rounding off figures in equations from six decimal places to three—might shift a projected weather pattern from a bright sunny day to a rainstorm. He immediately concluded that it would be impossible to predict weather for anything but the most immediate time period. His discovery became associated with "the butterfly effect," whereby a butterfly flapping its wings in Hong Kong might impact the weather in New York City. Today, you can think of the spread of a particular flu strain from its origin to countries around the world in a matter of days and the compounding of a global financial crisis from one institution to another as further examples of this phenomenon. In summary, all things in our world are interconnected.

The first idea that "you cannot control events" is supported not only by the concept that all things are interconnected, but also by our common sense and common experience. In the 1972 Olympics held in Germany, the United States fielded what was thought to be the best team ever of 100 meter sprinters, and everyone was talking about a 1-2-3 sweep of the Olympic medals—a gold, a silver and a bronze. Guess how these sprinters actually finished. "Did they win the gold?" No! "Did they win the silver?" No! "The bronze?" No! In fact, no U. S. sprinter finished in the top ten. How did this happen? On the day of the qualifying heats, the U. S. team showed up in the afternoon, only to learn that their heats had been run in the morning, and the entire team had been disqualified. Their coach had misread the schedule. When interviewed on television, the athletes, one after the other, would say how they could accept losing in a race, but never to compete after preparing for years was just devastating.

The point is that no matter how hard you try, how well you prepare, you cannot control all of the variables to assure a specific result. Something can still go wrong. At the 1972 Olympics, the butterfly effect was "a schedule read incorrectly."

This brings us to the second idea that "you can make a difference." This thought is merely viewing the butterfly effect from a different perspective. In the first instance, the butterfly keeps you from controlling events. With the second idea, you become the butterfly—influencing not only events directly around you, but potentially over a much broader landscape.

A movie titled *Lorenzo's Oil* tells the true story of a boy named Lorenzo who contracts a rare degenerative brain disease called ALD, which over a period of years destroys brain function leading to death. Lorenzo's parents, Augusto and

Michaela Odone, are told by the doctors that there is no cure for the disease and no hope for Lorenzo. They ask if any research is being done on the disease. The doctors say "No" because the disease is so rare there is no funding for it. But the Odones do not simply accept this fate. They head for the library at the National Institute for Health. There, they discover that, while there was some research relevant to ALD, none of the researchers were aware of the others' findings. To bring the researchers together, the Odones sponsored the first international conference on ALD. The conference led to the idea of a potential solution, which the Odones, through sheer perseverance, shepherded through to the development and trial production phase. After several iterations, a formula was found that arrested Lorenzo's deteriorating condition. It did nothing, however, to correct any of the previous damage done. The Odones shared their results with the parents of other ALD boys, who then put pressure upon the FDA to approve what became known as "Lorenzo's Oil." The time taken to create this drug and have it approved was less than three years and at a minimal cost. A typical new cure for a disease would take ten or more years and hundreds of millions of dollars.

The Odones show us that individuals can make a difference. But, were they able to control events? Clearly not. If they were, they would have cured their son the first day that he experienced this disease. However, Lorenzo lived many years longer than his doctors thought possible. Moreover, hundreds of boys treated soon after the onset of this illness are now leading near normal lives. The Odones could not control events, but they could make a difference—a difference for a better world. They became "the butterflies flapping their wings."

The observation that you cannot control events, but that you can make a difference has two implications. First, luck—

that is, events outside our control—has a lot to do with what happens in our lives. In the previously-mentioned book, *The Black Swan,* Nassim Nicholas Taleb makes the point that contrary to what we might normally think, the most important circumstances in our lives are often the result of highly improbable events. American Woodmark had the good fortune of completing its acquisition of Boise Cascade's cabinet business on May 1, 1980. Had the closing been scheduled a month later, the transaction would have never occurred. In June, 1980, the Federal Reserve, in its effort to fight inflation, banned the type of leveraged-buyout financing that we needed to complete the purchase. We were lucky.

Since luck does play a role in our lives, we should not let hubris cloud our perspective when things go well. We should appreciate the fact that whatever talents we have and whatever efforts we apply, luck—good luck—also plays a role. On the other hand, when things don't go so well, and we have done our best, we shouldn't be so hard on ourselves. Luck—in this case, bad luck—also played a role. In my life, I have had things go very well, and I have suffered tragedies. Luck—or events I could not control—has played a role in both.

The second implication is that, "Seeking to make a difference in your life is a *choice.*" One person who has influenced my outlook on life is Viktor Frankl, author of the already cited *Man's Search for Meaning,* which describes his experiences in Auschwitz. He lost his wife and parents but managed to survive himself. He commented in the preface to the book:

> *Don't aim for success—the more you aim at it and make it a target, the more you are going to miss it. For success, like happiness, cannot be pursued; it must ensue, and it only does so as the unintended side-effect of one's personal dedication to a cause greater than oneself or as the by-product of one's surrender to a person other than oneself.[1]*

The Odones are examples of such dedication. While we cannot guarantee a specific result in our lives, we can create meaning by serving others and dedicating ourselves to causes greater than ourselves. You will have an untold number of opportunities to create such meaning in your lives. You can make a difference. The choice is yours.

QUESTIONS FOR REFLECTION

- Have the choices you have made and the effort you have extended played a role in your life? Has luck played a role?

- Where do you find meaning in your life?

RELATED CHAPTERS

- Essays: Imagine and Inspire: 69
            "What Do I Want?": 78

SECTION
3

SECTION 3

LESSONS

OVERVIEW

This section presents lessons that provide the education and training necessary to help make the vision of an exceptional organization a reality. The lessons are divided into four parts, corresponding to the presentation of the essays: "The Vision," "The Leader," "Processes and Tools" and "The Journey."

At the end of each lesson is a "Future Study" segment, which when completed will reinforce the learning. Also included is a cross-reference to related lessons and essays.

SECTION 3.1

THE VISION

OVERVIEW

This section presents three lessons that support the vision-related essays. The first, "Vision-Driven Organizations," shows how exceptional enterprises organize work both in the pursuit of their purposes and in the creation of business strategies that generate significant and sustainable cash flows. The second, "Culture," presents four elements that comprise a culture and shows how these elements influence behavior. The third, "Values," provides an understanding of the core values we live by and their universality across societies.

22

VISION-DRIVEN ORGANIZATIONS

This lesson provides a basic understanding of *what* it is that organizations do to achieve their purposes. It shows that exceptional organizations create visions that support their purposes and organize all activities around their achievements. It describes the creation of business strategies for sustainable cash flows, the importance of aligning work and the need to continuously evaluate reality to assure that actions taken continue to be appropriate.

This material is based upon William J. O'Brien's book, *The Soul of Corporate Leadership* and by Robert Fritz's, *The Path of Least Resistance for Managers.*

ORGANIZING PRINCIPLE

The *vision-driven* organizing principle is the pursuit of ambitious end results which, when achieved, support the entity's purpose. All activities are focused upon the achievement of the organization's visions, and all decisions are made based upon the merits of whether or not they support them. An important aspect of the vision-driven organization is that it defines not only the work to be done but also the work to be eliminated.

In the absence of a vision-driven organizing principle, actions are frequently independent of the organization's purpose. This is especially true when the motivation for action shifts to meeting the needs of those higher up in the hierarchy. When this occurs, decisions are not made on their merits, but rather to please the boss. This leads to a lack of organizational effectiveness resulting in wasted or misguided efforts.

The vision-driven organizing principle is based upon a discrepancy between what we want—our *vision*—and what we have—our *current reality* relative to this vision. This discrepancy creates tension which leads to action to resolve the tension. This tension is resolved once the vision becomes the reality. As shown in Exhibit 22.1, work is organized into a hierarchy throughout the organization where actions at the highest level to achieve the organization's purpose become visions at succeeding lower levels, where more specific actions are taken. For example, the action steps for Level I become visions for level II. The actions for Level II then become visions for Level III.

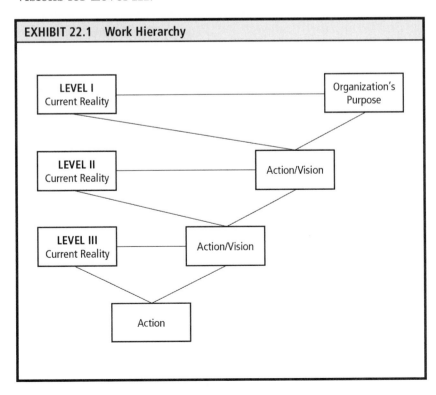

EXHIBIT 22.1   Work Hierarchy

Organizing work on a level-to-level basis assures that all actions necessary to achieve the organization's purpose are clearly established and are organized according to whoever is responsible for their achievement.

As part of the 1995 Vision, American Woodmark became a *vision-driven* organization. Goals at various levels in the hierarchy were reflected in scorecards, which consisted of performance expectations necessary to support the next higher level in the hierarchy. This approach focused work on only those activities that were essential for moving the organization forward and was substantially superior to our previous work processes. With the success of the 1995 Vision, the company created a 2001 Vision and subsequent visions for 2007 and 2013.

BUSINESS STRATEGY

One action step at the highest level of the organization is the creation of its *business strategy*, which along with other action steps, supports the organization's purpose. A business strategy, also referred to as a *business model*, is the vehicle by which organizations generate cash flow—either in the form of profits or, as some non-profits prefer to call it, "excess revenues over expenses." By doing so, for-profit organizations create wealth for owners, while non-profits generate cash reserves—the equivalent of wealth—to be held by them for the public good. Viable business strategies create competitive advantages; meaning that customers, clients and benefactors value their products, services or causes more than the offerings of competing organizations. For enterprises to be sustainable, they need to maintain or increase their competitive advantages over time.

THE DYNAMICS OF A BUSINESS STRATEGY

A business strategy is based upon the interrelationship of three elements: clients, providers and competitors. If what the provider offers matches what clients want, both parties benefit. The provider earns positive cash flow, and clients gain value by procuring the offering. Exhibit 22.2 illustrates this principle. The greater the intersected area, the greater the potential value creation for both parties.

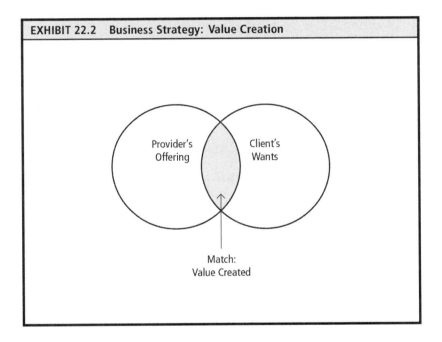

EXHIBIT 22.2   Business Strategy: Value Creation

Provider's Offering

Client's Wants

Match: Value Created

As the value accruing to the provider increases, however, so will the likelihood that competitors will want to capture some of that value by providing an alternative offering to clients. If they do, the original provider will see its value diminish as clients procure competitors' offerings. Exhibit 22.3 demonstrates these relationships.

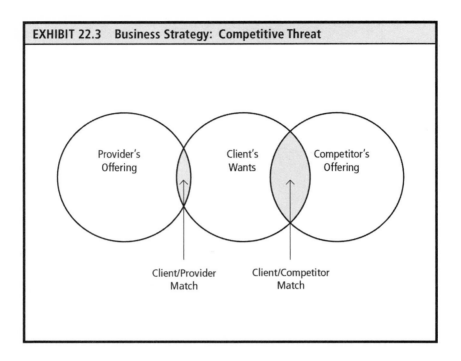

EXHIBIT 22.3   Business Strategy: Competitive Threat

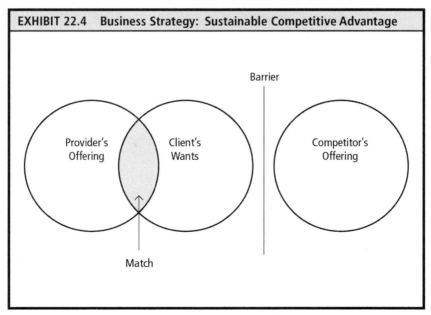

EXHIBIT 22.4   Business Strategy: Sustainable Competitive Advantage

The key to creating a business strategy is not only to create a viable business transaction, but also to maintain this relationship over time. To do this requires some mechanism that acts as a barrier to protect the provider's relationship with its clients from competitors as illustrated in Exhibit 22.4.

The challenge for the provider is twofold—to increase the value of the client/provider match, the intersected area in Exhibit 22.3, and to strengthen the barriers, as shown in Exhibit 22.4, that block the incursion of competitors upon this client/provider relationship. Successful business strategies do both.

CREATING A BUSINESS STRATEGY

A starting point in the creation of a business strategy is the consideration of a checklist of questions relative to each party and their interrelationships.

CLIENTS

- What offerings do clients want?

- How high a price can they pay and still receive value for themselves?

- What is the number of potential clients—the size of the market?

- Can the market be segmented by more focused, desired offerings?

- How can clients learn about the offering?

- How can clients get the offering?

- What will motivate them to buy?

- How quickly are client desires subject to change?

PROVIDERS

- What offerings can they provide?

- What offering price can they accept and still receive value?

- What is the minimum quantity they can provide and still receive value for themselves?

- What are their capabilities—market research, offering development, productive capacity, human resources, financial assets and other relevant capabilities?

- What impact would the providing of the offerings have on any other aspect of the organizations' businesses?

- Are there any limitations that would hinder the development and delivery of the offerings to clients?

COMPETITORS

- Can competitors develop offerings of equal or greater value than that of the providers and still receive value for themselves?

- What offering price can competitors accept and still receive value?

- What is the minimum quantity they can provide and still receive value?

- What are the competitors' capabilities—market research, offering development, productive capacity, human resources, financial assets and others relevant?

- What impact would the providing of the offerings have on any other aspects of the competitors' businesses?

- Are there any limitations that would hinder the development and delivery of competitors' offerings to clients?

CLIENT/PROVIDER RELATIONSHIPS

- Is there a match between what clients want and what providers can deliver?

- How long is this match likely to last, given the potential changing desires of clients?

- Is the potential value for providers significant enough to warrant the creation of businesses to provide these offerings?

COMPETITOR/CLIENT/PROVIDER INTERRELATIONSHIPS

- Can providers create barriers such that competitors are unable to disrupt the client/provider relationships?

- Can providers create business strategies that generate significant and sustainable cash flow for their enterprises?

There must be satisfactory answers to the above questions to create an adequate strategy. A simple example is the decision as to whether or not to open a lemonade stand. Do people want lemonade? What will they pay for it? How many people will walk by? What will it cost to provide the lemonade? Will there be enough profits to warrant opening the stand? What are the capabilities necessary for providing the offering? If a stand is opened now, will it preclude someone else from opening a similar stand nearby? While the issues impacting such a decision are straightforward, for more complex situations a significant amount of time and effort will be required.

The creation of a business strategy is more art than science. There is no formula. The principles apply to organizations large and small and for-profit and non-profit. Since 1983, American Woodmark has had essentially two different strategies. From 1983-1988, the company gained a competitive advantage by being the only manufacturer in the country which, as a result of its network of distribution centers, could deliver kitchens within two weeks of order placement. This ability was particularly important to home centers which wanted to offer consistent programs across the country. This strategy evolved naturally as we took steps to meet customer needs. Our second strategy was developed as part of our 1995 Vision which, while retaining the ability to offer kitchens with two-week lead-times, also significantly expanded our ability to provide both greater product variety and multiple brands. In contrast to our prior strategy, this one resulted from the insight inspired by the reading of a business publication. Although modified over time, it has served the organization well for the past twenty years.

Once a business strategy is created, it will be necessary to continuously monitor the changing reality among clients, the provider and potential competitors. If the dynamics that led to the strategy's creation change, then it may be necessary to adjust the business strategy as appropriate.

EXECUTION

The vision-driven organization executes all activities, including its business strategy, by creating a hierarchy of descending actions down through all levels in the organization. Each action supports the achievement of a vision. To assure their attainment, performance measurements are taken to determine progress and where necessary modifications are made. By doing so, the execution of work throughout the organization is self-correcting, increasing the likelihood that the organization's purpose will be achieved.

IMPLICATIONS FOR LEADERS

The following checklist is a guide for structuring work according to the vision-driven organizing principle.

CHECKLIST

1. Create a vision that supports the achievement of the organization's purpose and mission.

2. Examine the organization's current reality relative to this vision.

3. Develop high-level action steps that, if achieved, will take the organization from its current reality to its vision.

4. As one of the highest-level action steps, create a business strategy that enables the organization to generate a significant and sustainable cash flow.

5. Develop a hierarchy of lower-level action steps down through all levels of the organization.

6. Eliminate work that is not needed to support the vision.

7. Measure performance and modify actions as necessary.

8. Achieve the vision.

SUMMARY

"Vision-driven" is one of the four organizing principles of an exceptional organization. Such an entity organizes all work around the achievement of a vision in support of its purpose. It creates a hierarchy of work descending down through all levels of the organization. It measures its performance against its desired results and modifies its actions as necessary to achieve its vision. One of the highest-level action steps is the creation of the organization's business strategy, which enables the entity to generate a sustainable cash flow.

FUTURE STUDY

- For your organization, address each of the questions in the checklist listed for creating a business strategy. Answer whether or not you believe your organization's existing business strategy is viable and sustainable.

- If your organization's strategy is not adequate, can you develop a plan to modify it, so that it may become viable and sustainable.

RELATED CHAPTERS

- Essays: To Be Exceptional: 60
           Yes, Even for Non-Profits: 93

- Lesson: Working in Alignment: 244

23

VALUES

This lesson provides an understanding of values—those that are mere preferences and those that are core to our lives. It describes how individuals can develop their core values and the importance of these being consistent with those of the organization. It presents a desired governance structure for exceptional organizations that is based upon society's highest principles.

BACKGROUND

This material is based upon the works of; Rushworth M. Kidder in his books, *How Good People Make Tough Choices* and *Shared Values for a Troubled World* and William J. O'Brien in his books, *The Soul of Corporate Leadership* and *Character and the Corporation.*

WHAT ARE VALUES?

Webster's Dictionary defines a value as "that which is worthy of esteem for its own sake; that which has intrinsic worth." A value, therefore, is something that is an end in itself and not something desired as a step toward achieving another result. Under this definition, *freedom* is a value, but so is *eating chicken* if it is done for its own sake. In his book, *How Good People Make Tough Choices,* Rushworth Kidder distinguishes between what he refers to as *lettuce* values and those which help us answer the question, "What is right?"—which he calls *core moral values* or simply "core values." The word "moral" means that which is *good, right* or *ethical*. Kidder indicates that most people have an understanding of good— "they know it when they see it." We understand this at an inner level by a deep sense of intuition or judgment.

Because our values are intrinsically worthy and are ends in their own right, it follows that they are *freely chosen*. If they were not, they would be in the service of something else we desire. For example, individuals might be kind and respectful of others in the presence of someone of higher authority who would punish them if they were not; but in the absence of this higher authority, they might be mean-spirited. In this instance, these individuals would not "value kindness and respect for others," but would practice it only in the service of a higher desire—not to be punished. Although most people *understand* what is right or good, they do not necessarily *value* what is right or good. Those that truly do value kindness and respect behave accordingly regardless of the circumstances.

Before continuing, you may wish to stop and quickly list on a separate piece of paper what it is that you value. Include whatever comes to mind, without regard to whether it is a lettuce or core value. Continue until you have twenty to thirty items listed. Review your list and put an "x" before any item which you desire for its own sake, not because it helps you achieve another desire. For example, you might have listed "money," but for you its significance may only be that it helps you to get other things such as a home, a car or an education. Others might want money for its own sake. Finally, circle those items which you consider to be your core values. This exercise is not meant to be an all encompassing compilation, but rather a way for you to become more conscious of what you value.

DEVELOPING CORE VALUES— THE INDIVIDUAL

Most of us have established core values that guide our lives. For a few, this process has been an active choice with much study and reflection. For others, values have evolved over time without conscious awareness. Regardless of where we are in our moral development, there remains the possibility for us to continue developing our core values for as long as we live. In his previously mentioned book, *The Soul of Corporate Leadership*, William J. O'Brien described this endeavor as a striving for what he called *moral excellence*, which means "embracing, with vigor and commitment, age-old moral truths and pursuing their practice." Individuals who actively pursue the development of their core values will become more morally mature and will more likely approach a state of moral excellence.

We can outline the process for developing core values as follows:

- *aspiration*—Actively consider the core values and the resulting behaviors to which we aspire. Freely choose our desired values and expected behaviors.

- *current reality*—Examine our previously held values and resultant behaviors relative to our aspirations.

- *action*—Modify our behaviors according to our aspirations.

An example of this process is as follows:

AN EXAMPLE OF DEVELOPING CORE VALUES

- **Aspiration**—"After observing others, listening to people who I respect, and reflecting, I want to be honest in every way that impacts the well-being of another person."

- **Current reality**—"I rarely lie, but in the past I have sugar-coated the truth to make people feel better, when they would have been better served by my telling them the unvarnished truth."

- **Action step**—"When I am in these situations, I will consciously act to be completely candid."

By consciously examining our moral foundation, we will more likely live our lives according to our highest values and aspirations.

DEVELOPING CORE VALUES— THE ORGANIZATION

In his book, *How Good People Make Tough Choices*, Kidder states that organizations frequently attempt to answer the questions, "What are our core values?" or "What is right?" by adopting a code of ethics. The code is a guideline for behavior for the organization's members. A code is characteristically brief, not usually explanatory, and focused on core values. It can be expressed in a number of forms. He gives two examples:

EXAMPLES OF CODES OF ETHICS

Girl Scout Law

A Scout is:

- Trustworthy
- Loyal
- Useful
- Friendly
- Courteous
- Kind to Animals
- Obedient
- Cheerful

- Thrifty
- Clean in thought, word and deed

The West Point Honor Code

- A cadet does not lie, cheat, or steal or tolerate those that do.[1]

Each of these codes highlights behaviors that are valued and which answer the question of what is right.

In a second book, *Shared Values for a Troubled World*, Kidder describes interviewing twenty-four ethical leaders from sixteen countries. He posed the question, "If you could formulate a global code of ethics for the twenty-first century, what would be in it?" A number of the common themes that developed from the interviews were:

COMMON THEMES

- Love
- Truth
- Fairness
- Freedom
- Unity
- Tolerance
- Responsibility
- Respect for life.

Reading this list, you will likely conclude that these are familiar themes. They reflect values for living that have maintained relevancy over the ages.

While many organizations articulate their core values in either a code of ethics or a mission statement, the reality is that relatively few come close to behaving according to them. Some organizations use such statements to intentionally mask their real behavior and thus act fraudulently with their constituents. Others, however, have good intentions, but are simply overwhelmed by the structures within their organizations which preclude these intentions from coming to fruition.

Many organizations have as their primary organizing principle a *command-and-control* governance structure. With this structure, those higher in the hierarchy give orders to those below for execution. Those higher up control behavior by monitoring performance and administering rewards or punishments as appropriate. Under this structure, power and knowledge are typically hoarded at higher levels, and those below are focused upon "doing" more so than "thinking." This structure by its nature puts the emphasis upon pleasing the boss and acting in self-interest to gain rewards and avoid punishments.

While command-and-control based organizations may officially espouse acting according to core values, their governance structures usually hamper members from doing so. Moreover, other than declaring values in a code of ethics or mission statement, they typically have few supporting structures to foster higher moral formation.

An alternative governance structure, as described by William J. O'Brien in his book, *Character and the Corporation,* is one that is *value-based,* where members pursue both "self-interest" *and* "concern for others" and behave according to the merits of what is best for the organization. Power and knowledge are shared, and individual members hold themselves accountable for goal achievement and acting according to established values. While power is shared, those higher up in the organization maintain their hierarchical power and use it as necessary. Such a structure creates an environment that encourages personal growth both in skill development and moral formation.

On a spectrum with command-and-control governance on one end and value-based governance on the other, American Woodmark's 1995 Vision was an attempt to shift its structure to one that was more value-based. This desire stemmed in part from our new strategy, which required greater employee involvement in decision-making. We utilized broad-based training—incorporating many of the principles in this book—to help make this transition. This training helped people to better understand the merits of what was in the best interests of the organization so that they could act accordingly. Previous to this initiative, our mission statement values of *customer service, integrity, teamwork* and *excellence* were espoused but not well supported. A primary component of the 1995 Vision was to create processes that enabled the organization to live up to these principles.

INTEGRATING INDIVIDUAL AND ORGANIZATIONAL VALUES

Although organizations may adopt certain values or guidelines for behavior, their members can freely choose whether or not they will adopt these same values personally. While *behavior* may be coerced to a certain extent, no one can be coerced into adopting a personal value. An organization's members will be more effective and more satisfied when the match between their personal values and those of the organization are compatible.

Individuals and organizations will be most effective when the organization fosters, and individuals pursue, moral excellence. Where respective values are at cross-purposes, the individual and the organization may separate if the organization concludes that the individual's behavior is inconsistent with the organization's expectations or if the individual self-selects out of the organization. When the individual and organization share similar values, the intentions and actions of both parties are mutually reinforcing, enhancing both the achievement of the organization's purpose and the personal growth of its members.

IMPLICATIONS FOR LEADERS

The following checklists serve as guides for both individuals and organizations for developing and acting according to their core values.

CHECKLISTS

For Individuals:

1. Ask, "What are my core values and resulting desired behaviors?"

2. Determine current behaviors relative to those desired.

3. Take action to behave more in line with one's core values.

4. Measure performance and modify actions as necessary to achieve desired results.

For Organizations:

5. Establish the organization's purpose and mission.

6. Establish the organization's core values that will guide behaviors in the achievement of its mission.

7. Form a value-based governance structure whereby members hold themselves accountable for acting according to the organization's aspirations, values and expected behaviors.

8. Put in place mechanisms to correct behaviors that are not consistent with the organization's expectations.

SUMMARY

A value is that which is worthy of esteem in its own right. Core values help us answer the question, "What is right?" Values cannot be forced. They are freely chosen. However, they can be developed. Organizations frequently state their values in a code of ethics or mission statement. While many organizations espouse ethical values, relatively few live by them. Value-based organizations are the exception. They act according to what is best for the organization, guided by society's highest principles, and they foster the moral development of the individual.

FUTURE STUDY

● Ask yourself, "Do I want to pursue the development of my core values?" If you answer, "yes," use the "aspiration," "current reality," "action steps" tool as a methodology to develop one or more of them.

● If you have been associated with an organization that has espoused behaving according to ethical principles, evaluate whether the organization's behavior in practice is consistent with these principles.

RELATED CHAPTERS

● Essay: Nice Guys Finish Last: 54

● Lessons: Culture: 150
               Human Motivation: 225

24

CULTURE

This lesson explains the nature of cultures in organizations and their importance in shaping behavior. It describes one type of culture that acts as a key organizing principle for the creation of exceptional organizations.

DEFINITION

Webster's Dictionary gives two definitions for a "culture:"

- the customary beliefs, social norms and material traits of a racial, religious or social group

- the integrated pattern of human knowledge, belief and behavior that depends upon man's capacity for learning and transmitting knowledge to succeeding generations.

These definitions relate to a range of social groups, institutions and societies. We can adapt these definitions specifically for organizations by defining a culture as the *values*, *beliefs*, *traditions* and *processes* that guide behavior, or more simply, *how we do things around here*. This definition is illustrated in Exhibit 24.1. When interconnected, the organization's values, beliefs, traditions and processes form its culture.

FOUR ELEMENTS

The four elements of a culture can be described as follows.

EXHIBIT 24.1 How We Do It

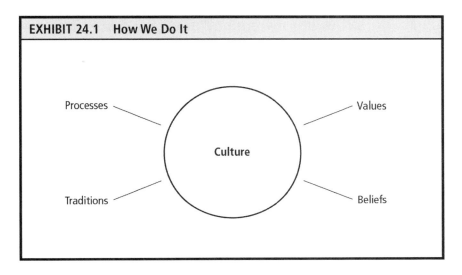

VALUES: As presented in the previous chapter, a value is something that is worthy of esteem for its own sake, something that has intrinsic worth. Of relevance here are *core values*, which guide people as to what is right. Examples of core values are "honesty," "responsibility," "freedom," "caring," "integrity" and "excellence." Values shape behavior. Someone who values "caring" may be more considerate of those who are suffering.

BELIEFS: Webster defines a belief as, "a state of mind in which trust or confidence is placed in some person or thing." People hold beliefs to be true, even though they may be unable to adequately prove their main contentions to others whom may or may not agree. For example, the belief that "people are basically kind" may be strongly held, but difficult to prove.

It is important to make a distinction between beliefs and *knowledge*. Plato said that knowledge is a "justified true belief." So a belief is knowledge, or the truth, if the believer has a justification that is reasonably plausible based upon evidence. Until the discoveries of Copernicus the statement "the sun revolves around the earth" could arguably be considered knowledge because there was reasonable and plausible evidence to that effect. Of course, that "knowledge" was debunked by Copernicus.

We can also distinguish between beliefs and *mental models*. A mental model is "our internal picture of how the world works." It is based upon the meaning we derive from the selective data we attend to. For example, the mental model "all our clients care about is cost" could be based upon data that showed that whenever new features were offered for a price premium, they were not purchased.

Beliefs and mental models are very similar and can often be used interchangeably. A subtle difference is that people who hold mental models more frequently think that their mental models are knowledge or "the truth," because they think that they have "proven" their position. People who hold beliefs by "placing trust or confidence in a person or thing" are less likely to think that their beliefs are the truth, because a belief by definition implies that the truth is not known, otherwise it would not be a belief in the first place.

TRADITIONS: We can define traditions as the handing down of information, beliefs and customs by word of mouth or by example from one generation to another without written instruction. Examples of traditions in organizations are:

- meaningful stories told about past experiences that become part of the entity's folklore
- ceremonies that remain consistent over time
- badges, medals, pins and other forms of recognition awarded in the present as in the past
- any symbolic behavior that links the present with the past.

Traditions shape behavior. Hearing stories about how people behaved in the past will influence people to behave in a similar manner in the future. Traditions can create a sense of being grounded, having roots and belonging.

PROCESSES: We can define processes as the policies, pro-cedures, methods, tools, programs and trainings used to do the work of the organization. Examples of processes, some of which are included in this book, are as follows:

- employee orientation programs
- decision-making tools
- meeting management procedures
- incentive plans
- strategy development plans
- working-in-teams guidelines
- absentee policies
- quality programs
- procedures for performance evaluation.

Processes are specifically designed to guide the behavior of individuals in organizations.

CREATING A VALUE-BASED CULTURE

Every organization has a culture. It may be deliberately crafted, or it may evolve without any conscious thought to its creation. Some cultures are weak in that there is little consis-tency in behavior from one part of the organization to anoth-er, while others are strong, where behaviors are consistent across the enterprise. The culture may be highly functional in that it supports the organization's mission and values, or it may be dysfunctional and hinder the achievement of the entity's aspirations. Furthermore, a culture which may have been appropriate at one stage in an organization's life may be inappropriate for the entity's next stage.

Exceptional organizations have strong cultures whose governance structures are *value-based*, as described in the pre-

ceding chapter. Value-based governance structures empha-
size behaviors in accordance with the merits of what is best
for the organization. While this principle is easy to embrace
in principle, it is very difficult to put into practice. Fostering
such behaviors is an organizing principle around which the
culture is built. It requires a clear understanding of the organization's mission and values. It necessitates the sharing
of knowledge, the development of skills and the applications
of appropriate tools so that people have a basis for deciding
what has merit. It encourages the sharing of power within
boundaries set by those higher in authority so that people
have the freedom to take action. Finally, it requires that the
organization's members be *willing* to make the appropriate
choices, realizing that they will be held accountable for them
by both the organization's standards and their own sense of
what is right or wrong.

With this approach, the four building blocks of the culture—values, beliefs, traditions and processes—are consciously chosen. The *values* are not only those that are universal to
society's highest principles, but also ones that are unique to the
specific enterprise—for example, "constant innovation," "superior customer experience" and "outstanding patient care."

An exceptional organization's *beliefs* are chosen not only
because they may best represent reality, but also because
they inform the organization's members on how best to act in
support of the entity's vision. An example would be, "Paying
more for the highest quality reduces costs in the long run."

Traditions are established to help the organization's
members to become grounded in those aspects of the enterprise's heritage that has allowed it to become what it is today.
These traditions not only give people a sense of place but also
reinforce those values and behaviors that have served the organization well in the past and which are expected to contin-

ue doing so in the future. Storytelling, award ceremonies and the celebration of milestones are examples of such traditions.

Organizations employ a number of *processes* to run their operations—the larger the entity, the greater the number. It is critical to the creation of exceptional organizations that each process be designed not just to accomplish a specific task, but to do so in a manner that also reinforces the overall framework of the culture. An example would be the use of common decision-making, communication and team-building tools across the enterprise. The processes included in this book are intended to support the creation of a value-based culture.

Cultures drive behavior. A company I have always admired as having a strong value-based culture is the department store, Nordstrom. I recall a sales clerk at one of its locations who, on what was perhaps the most hectic sales day of the year, cheerfully packaged and wrapped together with ribbon several related Christmas gifts. As we talked, she commented on how much she loved working at Nordstrom. I asked her, "Why?" Although I had this experience more than twenty years ago, I will never forget her response. She said, "You always get a fair shake." and, "There's always someone who cares."

IMPLICATIONS FOR LEADERS

The following points are relevant.

- Every organization has a culture, but the culture may or may not support the organization's purpose and mission.

- A value-based culture—one that holds both universal societal values and those specific to the organization—is critical to the formation of exceptional organizations.

- The desired culture must be consciously constructed with attention paid to all of its building blocks—values, beliefs, traditions and processes.

- Some existing cultural elements may no longer be appropriate while others may be required.

- Once established, the desired culture must be vigilantly safeguarded.

SUMMARY

An organization's culture has four key elements: its values, beliefs, traditions and processes. Cultures are important because they guide behavior. A value-based culture focuses behavior based upon the merits of what is best for the enterprise. Such cultures are critical for the formation of exceptional organizations.

FUTURE STUDY

- For organizations where you have been a member, make a list of its values, beliefs, traditions and processes. Examine your list and make another list of behaviors that are influenced by these key elements.

RELATED CHAPTERS

- Essay: To Be Exceptional: 60

- Lessons: Values: 141
            Mental Models: 210
            Cultural Change: 254

SECTION 3.2

THE LEADER

This section offers two lessons that show how organizations can put into practice the principles described in the essays on leadership. The first, "Leaders and Followers," describes the appropriate use of power and defines who leads and who follows and when individuals should be in one role versus the other. The second, "Leadership Styles for Decision Making," provides a framework for the leader's use of five alternative decision-making styles and describes when it is appropriate to use each.

25

LEADERS AND FOLLOWERS

This lesson provides an understanding of the behavior of leaders and followers. It describes motivations for appropriate use of power, followers' attitudes toward a direction and the scope of individual responsibility and accountability. It presents a new view for determining who leads and under what circumstances. This view provides a leadership framework integral to the formation of exceptional organizations.

DEFINITIONS

As previously mentioned, the word "leader" literally means "the one who walks ahead." If one is walking ahead, by implication there must be at least one other who follows, with the one in the lead setting the direction. Those who lead exist only to the extent that there are those who follow. Here we can define leaders and followers:

- **Leader**—one who pursues a particular direction and influences others to move in that direction

- **Follower**—one who is influenced by another to pursue a particular direction.

The direction pursued could be a literal direction with physical movement or any particular action or change in thought. With these definitions, who leads and who follows is based upon *behavior* and not upon any predetermined status or rank.

POWER

Our society values powerful people—those who are in control and who can make things happen. For all its importance, however, the principle of power is often misunderstood, principally because the word "power" has different meanings depending upon the context of its use. *Webster's Dictionary* provides two related but different definitions of power:

- "a possession of control, authority or influence over others"

- "the ability to act or produce an effect."

POWER AS CONTROL: The first definition describes a *relationship* between two parties, where the first party has the ability to constrain, coerce or influence the action of the second. The first party has freedom of choice, while the second's freedom is limited. With this meaning of the word, our society values those who have *power over* others. Those who are subject to such power are viewed as weaker and of less consequence. The king is valued more highly than his subjects.

POWER AS CAPACITY: The second definition describes *power as capacity*—the ability to take effective action. The capacity might be that of an individual acting alone, or it may result from an individual controlling the behavior of others. What is important is that the action be effective, not how it is taken. Our society values more highly those with greater capacity than those with less. A baseball player who bats .400 is more highly regarded than one who bats .280.

Oganizations of any type require both types of power. Imagine a sailboat race. The goal is to win the race. The captains are responsible for setting their courses and instructing their crews. They are continually monitoring wind changes and the position of their boats relative to others to make whatever major or subtle changes are necessary to create an advantage. They need *power as capacity* in the form of skills necessary to evaluate possible courses of action and to choose course directions. They also need *power over* their crews so that their orders will be followed. If they are not, there will be chaos. In addition, it isn't enough that crews be willing to follow directions, they must also have power as capacity to effectively perform their duties.

HIERARCHICAL POWER: Hierarchical power occurs when power, as control, is prescribed based upon a particular position or status. In our society, the formal governance of corporations is established by a series of laws. Shareholders, who are the legal owners of a business, choose a board of directors, who in turn choose a Chief Executive Officer to run the business. The CEO makes decisions and takes actions within guidelines established by the board. The board has hierarchical power over the CEO, who has hierarchical power over the rest of the company's employees.

SHARING POWER: Individuals who have hierarchical power may share this power with others. Ship captains delegate certain decision-making authority, or power, to others as they think appropriate. Although power is delegated, captains are still responsible to their superiors for the effective running of their ships and the actions of any of their subordinates. If ships run aground, their captains are held accountable even if at the time they are off deck in their sleeping quarters. Furthermore, even though power may be delegated to others, it may be revoked at any time.

In the formation of American Woodmark, as described in the case study, I consciously chose to give up voting control of the company to my three cofounders if and when they decided to vote together in opposition to me. Why did I make this choice? First, I believed that by sharing hierarchical power that I would increase the likelihood that these individuals, whom I considered vital to the new enterprise, would want to join the organization. Second, I thought that the company would have a better chance of success. I had confidence in my leadership capabilities, and I did not think it necessary to retain complete *power as control* to accomplish what I desired or to hold my position. By taking this action, I intended to expand *power as capacity* for both my cofounders and the organization as a whole. I believed that this structure would heighten each cofounders sense of personal responsibility, because each knew that he had freedom of choice—by either agreeing with me or by acting in concert with the other two. I considered this voting-power structure to be a contributor to our success, especially during the 1980-1982 time period when we were concerned about the company's survival. During tough times, it is easy to find fault with a leader's direction, especially when one has no power to change things— the typical Monday morning quarterback. In our situation, we were aware that we all shared formal power for running the company, so each of us experienced a heightened sense of ownership and personal responsibility. During these tough times, instead of becoming alienated with one another, we actually became closer. Although we frequently disagreed, there was very little finger pointing; and we came to decisions we could all support, even though we individually might have preferred a different course.

APPROPRIATE USE OF POWER

There are two motivations for the use of power:

- **Self-focused leadership**—to focus solely upon the benefits to oneself

- **Servant leadership**—to serve a cause greater than oneself.

Self-focused leaders motivate followers based primarily upon rewards and punishments appealing to the followers' own self-interests. As a result, followers tend to behave to "please the boss." When such leaders' interests are in conflict with organizations' purposes and values, they will often resort to manipulation, deception and other wrongful behaviors for their own advantage. They are more likely to "know the truth" than to seek it, because they tend to see reality from the lens of what benefits them. They will oversee the professional development of followers only to the extent that they will benefit themselves. In summary, their own interests take precedent over those of the organization.

Servant leadership is characterized by behaviors based upon what is right for the organization. Servant leaders motivate followers by inspiring them to serve a cause greater than their own self-interests. When necessary, such leaders subordinate their own interests to the service of their organizations. They do what is right in accordance with their entities' purposes and values and are more likely to "seek the truth" than to "know it." These leaders nurture and mentor followers, and as a result both their organizations and their followers benefit beyond the horizon of their tenures. In summary, the organizations' interests take precedent over those of their leaders.

The right *motivation* for the use of power is servant leadership, not self-focused leadership. While both self-focused and servant leaders use both "power as capacity" and "power as control," servant leaders use their power to achieve their organizations' visions and to create environments where members freely choose to pursue them. Such leaders increase power as capacity for themselves and their organizations' members. Finally, they share power through delegation, while maintaining hierarchical authority. Servant leadership supports the organizing principles of "Inspiration" and "Right Person / Right Job" which are key elements of exceptional organizations.

LEADER AND FOLLOWER RELATIONSHIPS

We may categorize leader-follower relationships according to two criteria: first, whether the leader's influence is direct and *face-to-face* or indirect and more *distant*; and second, whether the leader has *hierarchical power* over the person influenced. Exhibit 25.1 shows examples of leader-follower relationships which fit each of the resulting four categories.

EXHIBIT 25.1 Leader-Follower Relationships		
	FACE-TO-FACE	DISTANT
HAS HIERARCHICAL POWER	Parents, Teacher, Boss	Grandparents, Principal, Boss's Boss
HAS NO FORMAL AUTHORITY	Siblings, Coworkers, Friends, Acquaintances	Sports Heroes, Authors, World Leaders, Celebrities

As infants, our parents are typically the first leaders we face. They have hierarchical power over us. As we grow, teachers and others soon join this group. Grandparents and school principals also have hierarchical power, but their leadership influence is less direct. Even though they have no formal authority, siblings, coworkers, friends and even one-time acquaintances may directly lead us. Furthermore, people whom we have never met personally and have no formal authority over us—sports heroes, authors, world leaders and celebrities—may significantly impact our thoughts, feelings and behaviors.

CHARACTERISTICS OF LEADERS AND FOLLOWERS

Our society places a higher value on leaders than followers. For example, there are a multitude of books written on how to lead, while there are very few on how to follow. Furthermore, we tend to ascribe different characteristics to leaders than to followers. Take a moment to complete the quiz in Exhibit 25.2.

EXHIBIT 25.2   Leader-Follower Quiz

Who are more likely to?

CHARACTERISTICS	LEADERS	FOLLOWERS	BOTH
Believe in a vision?			
Have skills and abilities?			
Have freedom of choice?			
Take responsibility?			
Hold themselves accountable?			

We typically think that leaders are more likely to exhibit these characteristics than are followers. Most of us, when asked to describe leaders we know, list people who have unique talents or skills that we admire. When asked to list followers, we frequently describe people whom we hold in lesser regard. Furthermore, many of us tend to label ourselves as either leaders or followers. These labels then serve as guides to our behavior, which in turn reinforce our self-images. The reality is that both leaders and followers have the potential to exhibit the characteristics listed above.

FOLLOWERS' ATTITUDE
TOWARD A DIRECTION

Jake Gosa, former CEO of American Woodmark, describes three beliefs about human behavior that are instrumental in our thinking about leaders and followers.

1. **People want to be led**—People have always organized around leaders, from tribal chief to kings, appointed leaders and elected officers. A leaderless group is a mob. Few people will choose anarchy over stability and predictability.

2. **People want to contribute**—People have a basic need to be valued for their contributions. Who goes home at night and says, "Honey, I screwed up the new product launch?"

3. **People want to be respected**—We are taught from childhood that, "all people are created equal" and that we have the same basic rights. We respond positively to an act of respect and negatively to an act of disrespect.[1]

How well these "wants" are met will impact how followers respond to a leader's direction.

In his book *The Fifth Discipline,* Peter M. Senge categorized five attitudes that followers may have toward a leader's direction:

- **Apathy**—neither for nor against the direction, no interest or energy and does what requires the least effort or discomfort

- **Noncompliance**—does not see the benefits of the direction and will not do what is expected

- **Grudging Compliance**—does not see the benefits of the direction, but fears the consequences of not following it, does the minimum necessary and voices disapproval along the way and may act maliciously by following the letter, but not the spirit of the law

- **Genuine Compliance**—sees the benefits of the direction and does everything expected and more

- **Commitment**—wants it, feels an ownership in the result and will make it happen.[2]

The movie, *The Bridge on the River Kwai,* provides a graphic portrayal of a group of people going through a transition from apathy to commitment.

THE BRIDGE ON THE RIVER KWAI

The commandant of a Japanese prisoner-of-war camp holding American and British soldiers during World War II is responsible for constructing a bridge over the river Kwai, using the prisoners as laborers. In one of the first scenes, prisoners are shown in sick bay faking illnesses to avoid work, followed by a scene where other workers are sabotaging the work effort on the bridge site by "accidentally" pulling over new sections of the bridge under construction, collapsing them into the river. The prisoners' attitudes clearly range from apathy to grudging compliance to malicious non-compliance. However, a new detachment of British prisoners are brought to the camp. The British Colonel leading this detachment refuses to follow an order by the camp commandant, because the order violates the Geneva Convention. The Commandant places the Colonel and his fellow officers in an "oven," a small metal enclosure exposed to full tropical sunlight, until he agrees to comply. While they are in there, the rest of the prisoners are now even less compliant, and the

*bridge construction falls significantly behind sched-
ule. After a number of days and no indication that the
Colonel will break, the Commandant frees the officers
and agrees that they need not work but can super-
vise their men. Having won a battle of wills by his
noncompliance, the Colonel now sees the building of
a "proper bridge" as a way to maintain discipline and
build morale among his troops. He enlists his fellow
officers and then the rest of the troops to support this
vision. As the movie progresses, we see a shift in the
behavior of the prisoners from those of avoiding or
sabotaging work, to grudgingly doing it, to full commitment. To complete the bridge on time both officers
and sick bay inhabitants eventually work alongside
the other men. When the bridge is finally completed
on time, the prisoners hold a celebration party. The
realization that they willfully helped the enemy's war
effort, if not completely forgotten, was at least suffi-
ciently rationalized.*

As this movie indicates, attitudes toward a particular direction can vary widely and can change over time. Followers
can hold any of these attitudes regardless of whether leaders
are face-to-face or distant or whether they have hierarchical
power or not.

WHO LEADS/WHO FOLLOWS—A NEW VIEW

As previously mentioned, the *traditional view* of who leads is
based upon position or rank. "Who leads" is fixed as long as
the formal leadership hierarchy remains intact.

The *new view* of who leads is based upon a range of factors including not only position or rank, but also knowledge,
skills and capacity. With this new view, the person who leads
is the one best able to lead in a particular situation. Since

virtually all of us at times "act to influence others to follow a particular direction"—our definition of leadership—it follows that *everyone is a leader*. Similarly, since we are all influenced at times by others to follow a direction, it further follows that *everyone is a follower*. For example, even though we may have rank over another party, to the extent that we so much as listen to them, and by doing so form a new opinion, we are acting as followers.

We can summarize these two views as follows:

TRADITIONAL VIEW	NEW VIEW
leaders lead	everyone a leader
followers follow	everyone a follower

The transition from the traditional view to the new view of *everyone a leader* and *everyone a follower*, although simple in concept, is profound in its implications. Important characteristics are as follows:

LEADERS:

- retain their hierarchical power

- when delegating, relinquish "power as control" to expand "power as capacity"

- must be willing to be challenged and accept the possibility that they might be wrong

- must be willing to follow.

FOLLOWERS:

- must have the courage to challenge leaders

- have a duty to obey leaders when doing so is not morally undermining or repugnant

- have a duty to disobey leaders when their behaviors are reprehensible

- must be willing to leave the organization.

BOTH LEADERS AND FOLLOWERS:

- are servants to the organization's purpose and values

- hold themselves responsible and accountable for their behaviors

- do not assume that they or other parties are automatically "right" or "know the truth"

- don't inherently see others in a one-down or one-up position

- think through the merits of decisions rather than make them for self-focused or bureaucratic reasons.

It is important to again state what *everyone a leader* and *everyone a follower* does not mean. It *does not* mean that everyone has equal leadership capabilities, nor does it mean the absence of a formal hierarchy of power or that the leadership role in a particular situation is up for grabs. With this orientation, those with greater leadership skills *do* tend to be higher up in the hierarchy, and hierarchical leaders *do* retain formal power over followers.

What this orientation *does* mean is that leaders, even those at the top of organizations, see themselves as personally responsible and therefore accountable to a higher authority, whether that be the organization's purpose, its value system or to their own consciences. Even though leaders have power over others, they see themselves as having a *choice* as to whether and how to share that power with followers. Sharing their power may lead to their becoming followers in particular situations.

With this orientation, followers also see themselves as having a *choice*—whether to follow and in what manner to follow. In his book, *The Courageous Follower*, Ira Chaleff stated that followers, like leaders, hold themselves personally responsible for their actions. They are prepared to challenge, question and offer suggestions. They do so without undermining the formal authority of their leaders to lead or relieving themselves of their responsibility to follow. While they respect the authority of their leaders, they do not blindly fall in step. Rather, they hold themselves accountable to the higher authority of the organization's purpose and values and their own sense of right and wrong, and they are prepared to disobey if they are asked to act in violation of this higher authority.

The orientation of *everyone a leader* and *everyone a follower* recognizes that organizations do and must have a chain of command that establishes hierarchical power. This orientation does not alter these relationships, but it does call upon the organization's formal leaders to be willing to forego their hierarchical power as they approach each situation. For example, a supervisor might ask a subordinate to unknowingly take an action that would be detrimental to the organization. In this case, the subordinate would challenge the supervisor's request, and the supervisor would defer to the subordinate upon concluding that this individual was more knowledgeable.

By adopting this orientation, organizations place a greater emphasis on power as capacity to accomplish the entities' vision and act according to its values rather than upon power as control to reinforce its established leadership hierarchy. In the previous example, the supervisor and the subordinate each see themselves as followers of the organization's purpose, with both subordinating themselves to the organization's vision and values. Although both parties are prepared to take either role, they both know that if there is a question about what action is in the best interests of the organization that the hierarchical leader has final authority.

It is critical to the formation of exceptional organizations that the *everyone-a-leader* and *everyone-a-follower* orientation be adopted, either explicitly or implicitly. Most people prefer working in this orientation. Those that do not, often select to leave the organization.

Servant leadership is critical to the creation of an *everyone-a-leader* and *everyone-a-follower* orientation. Self-focused leadership and servant leadership are two ends of the same spectrum. Many people have the potential to move up the spectrum toward a greater degree of servant leadership. Others, however, are too egocentric to ever serve a cause greater than their own self-interests. They are unwilling to consider their fallibility, intolerant of being challenged and unable to think of their subordinates in any way other than in a one-down relationship. To create this new orientation, organizations cannot retain such individuals—particularly those higher up in the organization's hierarchy.

IMPLICATIONS FOR LEADERS

The following points are relevant.

- The presence of servant leadership, and the absence of self-focused leadership, is critical to the organizing principles "Inspiration" and "Right Person / Right Job,"—both key elements of exceptional organizations.

- The *everyone-a-leader* and *everyone-a-follower* orientation meets the needs of people to be led, to make a contribution and to be respected.

- Leaders must first adopt the characteristics of this orientation before expecting others to embrace it.

- This orientation increases the quality of decision-making, develops the skills of both leaders and followers throughout the organization and inspires followers to greater commitment.

- This *every-one-a-leader* and *every-one-a-follower* orientation is an essential aspect of cultures that foster exceptional organizations.

SUMMARY

Leaders pursue a direction and influence others to follow. In doing so, they use both power as control and power as capacity. The proper motivation for the use of power is servant leadership, where leaders serve a cause greater than their own self-interests. Followers want to be led, to make a contribution and to be respected. The leader's behavior will impact the follower's attitude toward a particular direction.

The traditional view is that *leaders lead* and *followers follow*. The new view is *everyone a leader* and *everyone a follower*. This orientation benefits not only organizational effectiveness but also the personal growth and development of the entity's members. It is a key cultural element of exceptional organizations.

FUTURE STUDY

- Think about people who have had hierarchical authority over you. Where would you place them on a spectrum ranging from self-focused to servant leadership?

- Examine past situations where you have been a follower. What factors determined what role you played and your attitude toward the leader's direction?

RELATED CHAPTERS

26

LEADERSHIP STYLES FOR DECISION-MAKING

This lesson provides an understanding of a range of leadership styles for decision-making. It describes the factors leaders can use to determine which styles are most appropriate for particular situations. It indicates who should be involved in making a decision and describes the importance of this tool for creating exceptional organizations.

BACKGROUND

This lesson is an adaptation of principles included in a 1958 Harvard Business Review article, "*How to Choose a Leadership Pattern,*" written by Robert Tannenbaum and Warren Schmidt.

A QUESTION

Ask yourself if one of the following two leadership styles is better than the other.

- "I put most problems into my team's hands and leave it to them to carry the ball from there."

- "I believe in getting things done. Someone has to call the shots around here, and I think it should be me."

This lesson will help answer this question.

LEADERSHIP STYLES

We can summarize leadership styles into five categories:

- **Mutual**—leader allows the group to reach whatever decision it chooses within limits

- **Consult**—leader receives inputs, makes the final decision

- **Test**—leader presents tentative decision subject to change

- **Sell**—leader sells decision already made

- **Tell**—leader announces decision already made.

We can give an example of the five leadership styles in the planning of a picnic where the leader, who has decision-making authority, addresses subordinates as follows:

PLANNING A PICNIC

Mutual "Please plan our annual picnic. Set a time and place. Your only constraints are that it must take place within 10 miles of our location and be held some time in July."

Consult "I would like your suggestions on when and where to have our picnic, and I will then make a decision."

Test "What do you think of having our picnic at Clearbrook Park, on Saturday, July 15th?"

Sell "We will have our picnic at Clearbrook Park on Saturday, July 15th because everyone liked going there last year."

Tell "We will have our picnic at Clearbrook Park on Saturday, July 15th."

Take a moment and ask yourself which of these five leadership patterns you are most comfortable with. Now, consider which style you use most frequently when you are in a leadership role. People most frequently use the style they are most comfortable with.

FACTORS IN CHOOSING A LEADERSHIP STYLE

Is any one style better than any other? Depending upon the circumstances, one style may be appropriate while another may not. There are many factors to consider in choosing an appropriate leadership style. Key ones are as follows.

- **Time**—It takes time to involve followers in a decision. If time is critical, the leader may need to act quickly and unilaterally.

- **Knowledge and skill level of followers**—For followers to make a meaningful contribution toward a direction or decision, they must have knowledge and skills appropriate to the decision being made. In many instances, followers have unique knowledge that the leader does not have, making their input critical to choosing a proper direction.

- **Who is impacted by the decision**—If the decision impacts the followers more so than the leader or others outside the group, then more involvement by followers may be appropriate. The more the followers are impacted the more likely they will have relevant information for any decision. However, if the decision has a major impact outside the group, then the leader might want to maintain more control over the decision.

- **Degree of commitment required**—If it is necessary for followers to have a sense of commitment, rather than mere compliance for the direction chosen, it may be appropriate to give followers more involvement in the decision-making process.

- **Leaders' willingness to be influenced**—If leaders are unwilling to be influenced by the group regardless of their input, seeking their involvement wastes everyone's time. There are times when leaders believe so strongly in a direction that no issues raised by followers will cause them to change course.

While there is no one "best" leadership style that is universally applicable, one style may be more applicable than another given a particular set of circumstances. Effective leadership for decision-making requires first, the ability to choose the most appropriate style and second, the ability to competently use that style. While leaders may naturally prefer one style over another, it is important that they can play all the keys on the piano from "tell" to "mutual."

When leaders do use the appropriate style for the situation, followers are more likely to support the direction. When leaders are in the "tell" mode, followers can be committed to the direction if they believe that particular decision-making style is what the situation calls for. On the other hand, if a leader attempted to use a mutual pattern in the face of an emergency, it would immediately frustrate and alarm followers.

While leaders and followers are most effective when leaders use the appropriate style, they are least effective when leaders give the appearance of being in one style but are actually in another. Leaders who ask for input from followers but in reality have already made up their minds on a direction, will diminish any feelings of trust on the part of these followers. Unfortunately, leaders may not be aware of their own behaviors. At a conscious level, they may think they are seeking input when in reality they are not. Because most organizations have no language for describing leadership patterns, it is easy for such circumstances to arise. When leaders and followers learn about leadership styles, everyone develops a conscious awareness of the technique, and the likelihood of a misunderstanding is diminished.

When American Woodmark's senior leadership team was first exposed to the concept of the five leadership styles, I had assumed that I acted mostly in a *consulting* or *mutual* mode. I was surprised to learn that my team's perception was that I more often feigned acting in these modes but was actually in a *sell* mode because my mind was already made up. From that time forward, I was more conscious of the style I was in and attempted to better project that style to others.

It is important to note that while the *immediate circumstances* will dictate the most appropriate leadership style, the leader has a strong influence over what these circumstances will be. Some leaders will never allow their followers to gain enough knowledge and skill to participate in a decision, while others will continually strive to help followers develop and grow. Those leaders who do will create an environment which fosters increased capabilities, freedom and responsibility on the part of their followers. Exhibit 26.1 shows that as we create circumstances which allow us to move from *tell* to *mutual* as the most appropriate style, we reduce the use of authority used by leaders and increase freedom for followers. By doing so, followers will more likely be committed to achieving the organization's purpose.

WHO NEEDS TO BE INVOLVED?

A factor in choosing the appropriate leadership style is the leader's understanding of who needs to be involved and how they might impact or be impacted by the decision. There are four categories of people to consider:

- **Decision-makers**—those whose input is required to actually make the decision

EXHIBIT 26.1   Leader and Follower Behavior

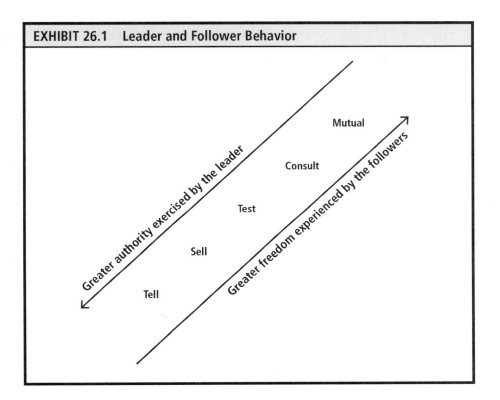

- **Technical experts**—those who aren't directly involved in making the decision, but whose expertise is needed by the decision-makers

- **People who need to be informed**—those whom will be impacted by the decision but will not have a voice in making it

- **Any person who has veto power**—those not directly involved in making a decision but who have veto power.

Very often, there is confusion about the roles of each party to a decision. By clarifying roles, the decision process will be more effective and efficient.

IMPLICATIONS FOR LEADERS

Key points are as follows.

- Typically, leaders are unaware of the leadership patterns they use in making decisions.

- By becoming aware of their patterns, leaders can increase their skill in using the most appropriate styles in particular circumstances.

- Better use of leadership patterns leads to better decision-making and a greater commitment on the part of all involved.

- By enabling followers to increase their knowledge and skills, leaders create an environment that allows followers to more fully participate in the decision-making process—to the benefit of the organization and their own growth and development.

- By making everyone in the organization aware of this decision-making process, collective learning of this methodology is significantly enhanced.

- The use of this process is a key tool supporting the creation of exceptional organizations.

SUMMARY

There are five leadership styles: *tell*, *sell*, *test*, *consult* and *mutual*. Decisions are best made when leaders choose the most appropriate leadership style for the particular situation. Decisions are less effective when leaders choose an inappropriate style. Over time, leaders can affect the circumstances surrounding decisions leading to greater freedom for followers and thus a higher level of commitment. The effective use of leadership styles for decision-making is a key building block in the formation of exceptional organizations.

FUTURE STUDY

- Prioritize the five leadership styles according to how often you employ them. Then, position the five styles according to your comfort using them. Note whether there is a relationship between the styles you use and your comfort level.

- Before you begin a decision-making process, consciously note which leadership style you think would best be used and then use this style, even if you are not initially comfortable with it. After making the decision, review how well you used it.

- If you are learning these skills as part of a group effort, post the leadership style continuum on the wall during decision-making deliberations. At the end of the session, review the effectiveness of the leadership styles used.

RELATED CHAPTERS

- Essays: Everyone a Leader: 73
             A Bad Plan Poorly Executed: 110

- Lesson: Leaders and Followers: 158

SECTION 3.3

PROCESSES AND TOOLS

This section presents six lessons that describe specific techniques that an organization can adopt in the pursuit of becoming exceptional. The first, "The 7-Step Process," offers a universal tool for doing work applicable to most any situation. The second, "Meeting Management," provides a format and instructions for conducting effective and efficient meetings. The third, "Understanding Discourse," highlights the distinction between two types of discourse, discussion and dialogue, and when each is appropriate. The fourth, "Mental Models," shows the power of our internal pictures of how the world works and how we can become more aware of these pictures and hold them up to scrutiny. The fifth, "Human Motivation," describes the nature of human behavior and how leaders can be sensitive to what motivates followers. Finally, "Working in Teams," shows the importance of highly effective teams in the creation of exceptional organizations.

27

THE 7-STEP PROCESS

This lesson presents the 7-Step Process as a method for individuals and organizations to create the results they truly desire. It describes the universality of the tool and its power in application.

BACKGROUND

As previously mentioned, Robert Fritz, a music composer by training, studied how people in the arts actually created their works. What he found was that regardless of the discipline—songwriting, sculpture or painting for example—creators consistently followed the same process. He also found that while they were able to effectively use this creative process in their professional endeavors, they typically did not apply this approach to other aspects of their lives. Fritz discovered that the creative process was in fact applicable far beyond an artist's specific discipline and, furthermore, that it could be learned. In his book, *The Path of Least Resistance,* he describes how to apply the creative orientation to all aspects of an individual's life. The 7-Step Process is an adaptation of Fritz's description of the creative process configured in a format more applicable to organizations.

METHODOLOGY

The process is as follows:

THE 7-STEP PROCESS

1. Create a Vision	Clearly picture the results you desire.
2. Understand Current Reality	Know where you are today.
3. Take Action	Act in a way that moves you from your current reality toward your vision.
4. Measure Performance	Track your progress.
5. Modify Actions	Change your behavior when necessary to get back on track.
6. Achieve Results	Accomplish your results by making your vision your new reality.
7. Create a New Vision	Clearly picture a new result you desire.

The power of the 7-Step Process comes from *structural tension*, what Fritz characterizes as an impetus for human action. Structural tension is caused by the discrepancy between what we want—our desired result—and what we have—our current reality. When we picture both the vision and the current reality at the same time, the tension created impels us to take appropriate action to resolve the tension. Exhibit 27.1 shows these relationships.

Once actions are initiated, we can measure performance relative to expected progress toward our vision, and we can modify our actions as necessary until we achieve our desired result. At this point, we can create a new vision.

Think of a child learning to ride a bicycle. The child's vision is to have the ability to ride, but the current reality is an inability to do so. The resulting discrepancy leads to tension which leads to action—practicing how to ride by balancing, pedaling, steering and braking. Unfortunately, the child makes many false steps along the way—falling over and crashing—until by continually modifying his or her actions the skill is eventually learned, and the vision is achieved. Once the tension is resolved, the child creates a new vision, such as riding the bike to school.

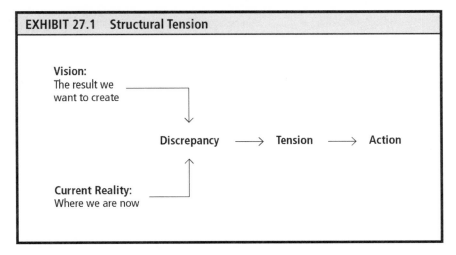

EXHIBIT 27.1   Structural Tension

Since the act of learning to ride a bicycle seems natural and intuitive, we are typically not aware of the process by which we do it. The 7-Step Process, however, makes users *conscious* of this natural process and thereby enables them to apply this technique to a variety of situations. Exhibit 27.2 shows a schematic representation of this process.

THE UNIQUENESS OF THIS TOOL

There are a multitude of management tools that start with the creation of a vision and then go on to develop action steps in one manner or another to achieve it. What these techniques fail to include, however, is any mention of *current reality* as part of the process. By so doing, they make it much more difficult to create structural tension and thus the impetus to act. Furthermore, the action steps taken may be either inadequate or inappropriate. To book a flight to Chicago, it is important to know that your starting point is Atlanta, not Los Angeles.

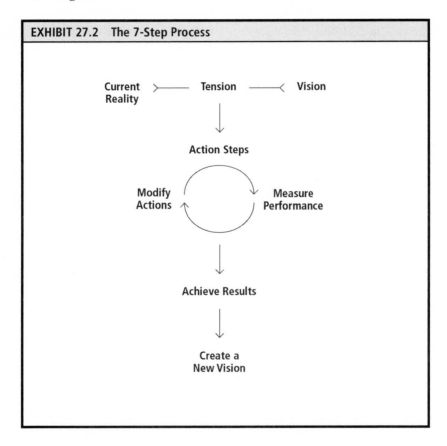

EXHIBIT 27.2   The 7-Step Process

While many tools start with a vision and ignore current reality, others do just the opposite. They focus on current reality and never consider what is truly desired. Current reality is typically described as a problem and the solution is to make the problem go away. While we frequently do want to see problems go away, focusing our energy on the problem simply ignores the possibility that what we often want is something entirely different. For example, a product may have a quality defect, and under a problem-solving approach we would go about fixing the defect. What we may really want, however, is an entirely new product to replace the existing one, making the fixing of the problem irrelevant. Finally, not articulating a vision impedes the creation of structural tension between our vision and current reality.

Another unique aspect of the 7-Step Process is that it turns upside down the way we traditionally allocate time to do work. When faced with a situation, we traditionally spend the majority of our time considering alternative action steps. It is only when those actions are not obvious that we go back, but not explicitly, to reconsider what we want and our current status. It may be considered macho to have "a bias toward action," as some authors articulate, but all too frequently it leads to extensively modifying actions when the first ones fail. With the 7-Step Process, practitioners spend most of their time creating the vision and understanding current reality. Once this is done, the action steps become relatively obvious. Furthermore, there is less time needed to modify actions to achieve results.

CHECKLISTS FOR EACH STEP

The following outlines are checklists to help guide each step.

CREATE A VISION

- Slow down your thinking.

- Ask, "What do I want?"

- Disregard others' expectations.

- Disregard "what is possible."

- Start with a blank page.

- Form a picture.

- Clarify the picture.

- Let your vision come alive.

- Break down extremely ambitious visions into a series of more manageable sub-visions.

- Hold your vision.

- Gain team agreement as appropriate.

UNDERSTAND CURRENT REALITY

- Slow down your thinking.

- Ask, "What is the relevant data?"

- Be aware of your biases.

- Separate fact from opinion.

- Picture patterns within the data.

- Understand how the key elements interrelate.

- Seek the truth, don't "know it."

- Gain team agreement as appropriate.

TAKE ACTION

- Generate possible actions.

- Decide on actions to take.

- Ask, "Do these actions address all of the discrepancies between current reality and the vision?"

- Prioritize the actions.

- Set dates for completion.

- Assign responsibility for achievement.

- Ask, "If we take these actions successfully, are we likely to achieve our vision?"

MEASURE PERFORMANCE

- Track whether action steps are successfully completed on time.

- Measure progress relative to milestones that lead toward the achievement of the desired result.

MODIFY ACTIONS

- Take new initiatives to complete action steps that are behind schedule.

- Reprioritize steps as necessary to compensate for uncompleted actions.

- If milestones are not achieved on time, even though action steps are on track, then re-evaluate your plan and add additional action steps as appropriate.

ACHIEVE RESULTS

- Don't confuse completing all action steps with achieving the desired result.

- Measure achievement by asking, "Is the vision now the reality?"

CREATE A NEW VISION

- With the vision achieved, the original structural tension is dissipated, and new desired outcomes will come forward for consideration.

APPLYING THE 7-STEP PROCESS

INDIVIDUAL TASKS: The simplest application of the 7-Step Process is for addressing tasks that can be completed by users on their own. These tasks can be either work-related or relevant to users' personal lives. A Personal Action Plan is a form for use on such projects. An example of a completed form is included in Exhibit 27.3.

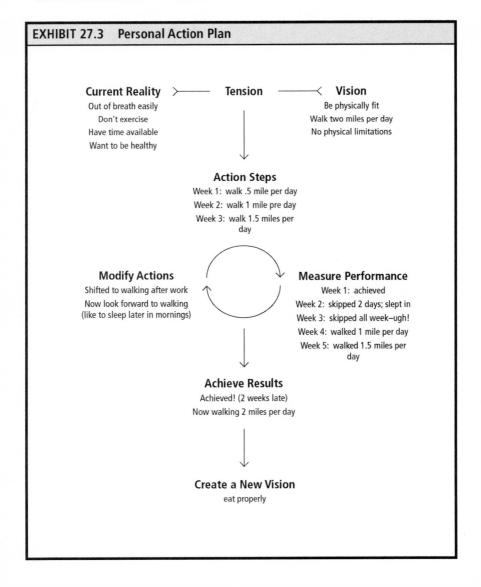

EXHIBIT 27.3   Personal Action Plan

Current Reality >——— **Tension** ———< **Vision**
Out of breath easily   Be physically fit
Don't exercise   Walk two miles per day
Have time available   No physical limitations
Want to be healthy

Action Steps
Week 1: walk .5 mile per day
Week 2: walk 1 mile pre day
Week 3: walk 1.5 miles per
day

Modify Actions   **Measure Performance**
Shifted to walking after work   Week 1: achieved
Now look forward to walking   Week 2: skipped 2 days; slept in
(like to sleep later in mornings)   Week 3: skipped all week–ugh!
Week 4: walked 1 mile per day
Week 5: walked 1.5 miles per
day

Achieve Results
Achieved! (2 weeks late)
Now walking 2 miles per day

Create a New Vision
eat properly

The following story was told by Brian Allen of Project HOPE and shows one person's application of this process.

LOOKING FOR A HUSBAND

Last year I trained members of our staff in Malawi, Africa on the use of the 7-Step Process. At the end of the session, I asked each of them to pair up with a co-worker and share their Personal Action Plans. As I walked around the room listening to the conversations and assisting when needed, I heard one young lady talking about looking for a husband. I walked over to that table and asked if I had heard correctly. She said that I had. I commented that this was the first time I had actually heard anyone use the 7-Step Process to manage their search for a spouse. She was very quick to correct me saying that her search for a husband was not her vision but one of her action steps. This led me to wonder what her vision was. I quickly thought that her vision must then be to have children. I asked if that was the case. "Oh no," she replied, "My vision is to have a car. If I have a husband he will buy me a car." We discussed this in the context of the 7-Step Process, and although I may have questioned the wisdom of her vision, she was following the process properly.

That following weekend I was still in country. On Sunday, after church services, I went to a local pizza parlor. I sat at a table that provided me with a vantage point to observe people entering the establishment. As I ate my pizza, who should walk in but this particular young lady, accompanied by a tall slender young man. The couple did not notice me. They ordered their food and sat outside under a parasol. They seemed to be infatuated with each other. As I left I walked by their table. Surprised, she took note that

*it was me and greeted me. I greeted her, and as she
looked at me I nodded over to the young man, leaned
down and asked her in a whisper if he was part of her
action plan. Embarrassed, she quickly began shaking
her head and said over and over, "Oh, no." The young
man seemingly had no idea as to what I was referring.
Due to her reaction I dropped the subject, bid farewell,
and wished them a good day.*

*When I returned to Malawi, I found that this young
lady was no longer with Project HOPE. Her partner for
the 7-Step Process exercise, however, was still there and
informed me that the young lady was coming by the office
to visit me. When she arrived she proudly informed me
that she was now married and now had a car. Her husband was in fact the young man from the pizza parlor.*

TEAM TASKS: The benefits of the 7-Step Process and the
value of creating structural tension become apparent when
the process is applied to team tasks. There is an immediate focus upon what the team wants to create, and any discrepancies in what people think the vision should be can be
highlighted and discussed until a shared sense of purpose
evolves. It is useful to record this vision on a flip-chart page
for everyone to see. Similarly, the key elements of current
reality can be recorded and placed on a page adjacent to the
one summarizing the vision. Only after there is agreement
on both the vision and the current reality should the team
consider possible action steps. As indicated earlier, these
tend to be quickly apparent as the discrepancy between the
vision and current reality becomes clear. The team can establish due-dates and assign responsibilities for achieving
each action and then set appropriate milestones for keeping
the project on track until the desired results are achieved.

AMERICAN WOODMARK'S EXPERIENCE

As previously mentioned, American Woodmark introduced the 7-Step Process as part of its 1995 Vision. The process was soon the primary method for doing work throughout the organization. Over time, it became the organizing principle for various other processes, such as scorecard development, individual and departmental performance-planning and appraisal, strategic planning and the creation of the company's six-year visions.

KEY ATTRIBUTES

The 7-Step Process is easy to learn, simple to use and powerful in application. Even for those just learning the process, it will likely deliver desired results more readily than those produced by proficient users of other methodologies. Mastery of the 7-Step Process, however, is a lifelong effort requiring practice, discipline and focus. But with this mastery comes an enhanced ability for individuals and organizations to create what they want.

IMPLICATIONS FOR LEADERS

Key points are as follows.

- Because of the universality of the tool and its effectiveness, the 7-Step Process can be used as the primary way for an organization to do work.

- As more people learn the process, the organization's collective skill level in its use increases dramatically, leading to even greater results.

- Other processes—employee orientation, training programs, performance planning and evaluations, strategy creation and budgeting, among others—can be developed utilizing the 7-Step Process.

- By utilizing this tool to help create a range of the organization's processes, this tool becomes a critical building block of the organization's culture.

SUMMARY

The 7-Step Process is a method for individuals and teams to create the results they truly desire. Since it is applicable to most any situation, it is of particular use as a primary tool for organizing work and getting things done. It is easy to learn, simple to use, powerful in application, but takes a lifetime to master. It can become a critical element in the creation of exceptional organizations.

FUTURE STUDY

- Utilize the Personal Action Plan to address situations which you can complete on your own. These can be either personal or work-related.

- Team with a partner who is also building skills with this process. Each of you can act as a consultant to the other. When acting as the consultant, use clarifying questions to test the adequacy of each step.

- If you are a team leader, use the 7-Step Process to address an organizational issue. You can do this even though no one else is familiar with the technique.

- In situations where a team is working together to build skills, designate one individual to act in a consulting role to test the adequacy of each step of the process.

RELATED CHAPTERS

28

MEETING MANAGEMENT

This lesson presents a standard format to conduct effective and efficient meetings. It describes materials needed, the creation of a visual record, ground rules and desired results.

STANDARD MEETING FORMAT

How would you characterize the meetings that you attend? Most participants are frustrated by the experience. The cartoon in Exhibit 28.1 exemplifies this frustration.

A standard format will foster effective and efficient meetings.

STANDARD MEETING FORMAT

- Icebreaker
- Review Agenda
- Set Expectations
- Content
- Next Step
- Review Expectations
- Feedback

EXHIBIT 28.1   The Joy of Meetings

"Today's meeting will be endless, with a half-hour break for lunch."

Each element is critical to the creation of a successful meeting.

ICEBREAKER: The purpose of the icebreaker is to break the ice, to get everyone to relate to each other and to participate immediately in the meeting. Icebreakers should be fun and should reduce tension, not add to it. The length of the icebreaker should be proportional to the length of the meeting. A one hour meeting should have no more than a two to three minute icebreaker, whereas a five-day meeting may have up to an hour.

REVIEW AGENDA: By reviewing the agenda, participants gain consensus about the purpose, focus and flow of the meeting. Agenda topics can be clarified and items can be either added to or eliminated from the agenda as appropriate.

SET EXPECTATIONS: Clarifying the participants' expected results of the meeting will further define its focus and flow and establish what must be accomplished for it to be successful. Expectations which are beyond the scope of the meeting can be identified at the start of the meeting, thereby reducing participant frustration later on.

CONTENT: The working purpose of the meeting is addressed in the sequence of the topics listed in the contents of the agenda. It is critical that meeting participants stay focused and not get diverted with subjects beyond the scope of the meeting.

NEXT STEP: It is important to determine the logical next step following this meeting. It may be a future meeting to follow up on agreed to actions, to establish additional action steps, or to create a new desired outcome. There may be no next step if the meeting's purpose has been achieved.

REVIEW EXPECTATIONS: By reviewing expectations at the end of the meeting, there is a recognition as to whether or not the participants' expectations have been successfully met. Often, if they have not, they can be addressed at this time.

FEEDBACK: The purpose of this segment is to learn how to improve future meetings, to enhance interaction among participants, to express emotions which have not previously surfaced during the meeting, to provide positive feedback and to provide constructive feedback appropriate to the group as a whole. Be sensitive to people who may view group feedback as threatening or counterproductive. It may be necessary for a group to share only positive feedback for several meetings before it is ready for constructive feedback. Discuss any concerns with the group prior to beginning the feedback segment. Give feedback that is critical of specific individual behavior on a one-on-one basis after the conclusion of the meeting.

MATERIALS NEEDED

The following general materials are needed, plus any other items unique to the meeting:

- agenda issued to participants in advance as appropriate, along with any preparation materials

- flip charts, markers and tape.

VISUAL RECORD: Recording information visually has several advantages. It helps to organize the flow of the meeting, it is a way to help create and capture common understanding and, it creates a record of the meeting which can then become the minutes.

- Prior to meeting, put the agenda on a flip-chart page.

- Record expectations, decisions made, action steps, unresolved issues, feedback and all other key information on flip-chart pages.

GROUND RULES: The following ground rules are applicable to all meetings:

- team logistics
  - arrive on time
  - start on time
  - end on time, unless the group formally agrees to extend the meeting

- conduct during the meeting
  - be respectful
  - be open and honest (this will require trust which cannot be mandated, but which must be developed over time)
  - confront issues not people

- one person speaks at a time

- decision-making
  - clarify how decisions will be made and whom outside the meeting may be needed for approval

- action steps
  - record actions to be taken along with the name of the person responsible for their achievement and a due-date for completion

- issues
  - catalogue unresolved issues on an "Issues" page— by so doing, the meeting can continue to progress while the issue is captured for future consideration

- conduct outside the meeting
  - maintain any of the team's agreed to confidences
  - represent the team properly in words, action and attitude.

ROLES: The following roles are necessary:

- meeting leader
  - arranges meeting room
  - establishes agenda
  - invites appropriate participants
  - keeps the meeting on task

- scribe
  - records notes preferably on a flip-chart page for all to see
  - translates notes into short form minutes
  - distributes minutes

- facilitative monitor
  - assists leader with keeping on task

   ○   reminds group when ground rules are broken.

FOLLOW UP: As soon as reasonable after the meeting, send a typed version of the information recorded on the flip chart pages as minutes to meeting participants.

DESIRED RESULTS

A successful meeting:

- starts and ends on time (or earlier)

- achieves the purpose of the meeting

- concludes with a common understanding of meeting results and assignments

- achieves the agreed upon expectations of the participants

- is efficient—time is well utilized

- provides for mutual support and respect among participants

- creates participant ownership in results

- increases the level of trust among participants.

INFORMAL MEETINGS

The principles of the standard meeting format can be applied to frame one-on-one in-person and phone conversations. A quick icebreaker is usually appropriate, if it is no more than a discussion of the weather. The agenda and expectations can be confirmed by establishing, "What do we want to accomplish?" The content and next step can then be addressed. Finally, feedback can be ascertained by asking, "Have we covered all the issues?" and "How do you feel about our result?"

AMERICAN WOODMARK'S EXPERIENCE

Establishing a rule that all organization meetings would follow the meeting-management process was the most visible first step in American Woodmark's cultural-change effort. Meetings were more productive, everyone was learning a new common language and people could see concrete changes for the better.

IMPLICATIONS FOR LEADERS

Key points are as follows:

- Meeting Management is a highly effective tool which can be easily learned and applied.

- For organizations that have ineffective meeting management skills, its application can generate quick benefits for limited costs.

- Because of these factors, it can be a very effective initial step in changing an organization's culture.

SUMMARY

The standard meeting format consists of the following elements: icebreaker, review agenda, set expectations, content, next step, review expectations and feedback. By following the format, not only will the meeting be effective and efficient, but participants who use this process regularly will likely have greater respect and trust in each other over time. Meeting Management is a key process supporting the culture of exceptional organizations.

FUTURE STUDY

- Use this standard meeting format to conduct formal meetings that you lead. Meeting participants do not need to be familiar with the format for the process to be effective.

- Use the tool informally to frame one-on-one in-person or phone conversations.

RELATED CHAPTER

- Essay: The Much Maligned Meeting: 82

29

UNDERSTANDING DISCOURSE

This lesson presents an understanding of two types of discourse—discussion and dialogue. It highlights the purpose, methodology and expected results of each.

BACKGROUND

This material is based in part upon the work of Peter M. Senge in his book, *The Fifth Discipline*. Senge in turn has drawn upon his conversations with David Bohm and from Bohm's writings to address these concepts.

DISCOURSE

People in organizations spend a considerable amount of time in conversations or *discourse*. An organization's success often depends upon the quality of these interactions. Traditionally, however, organizations are not conscious of *how* they converse, or even that there are two categories of discourse of benefit—discussion and dialogue.

DISCUSSION

Webster Dictionary defines *discussion* as "a consideration of a question in open and usually informal debate." Its purpose is to present and defend different views. Participants advocate their positions, and together they evaluate alternative thoughts, reducing these alternatives until a common position is established. The benefit of discussion is that there is usually a useful analysis of a whole situation. Thoughts converge on a conclusion or course of action, and decisions are made.

The problem with discussion is that when parties advocate their own positions, it is difficult for them to be open-minded enough to consider the merits of alternative positions. Frequently, decisions are made based upon who has formal power or better skills of persuasion, rather than on what is best for the organization.

Most organizations use discussion as virtually their only form of discourse. While it is appropriate when it is time to reach a decision, there are other situations, particularly where new insights are required, when discussion is inappropriate.

DIALOGUE

An alternative to discussion is *dialogue*, which Webster defines as "an exchange of ideas and opinions." Where the definition of discussion incorporates the concept of *debate,* dialogue does not.

The purpose of dialogue is to present individual views as a means to discover a new perspective not anticipated by any one party. Whereas discussion incorporates an element of competition and advocacy—that is one idea in opposition to another—dialogue encompasses cooperation, group learning and idea creation. Dialogue is particularly useful when the subject matter is complex.

In *The Fifth Discipline*, Senge describes Bohm's three conditions for conducting dialogue: assumptions are suspended, participants view each other as colleagues and a facilitator guides the discourse.

- **Assumptions are suspended**—Participants are each aware of their assumptions and are willing to hold them up to scrutiny. When presented, these assumptions are neither defended nor advocated, but are suspended to see if a better representation of reality is more appropriate to the situation.

- **Colleagues**—Participants see each other as colleagues, where the influence of hierarchy is eliminated. Initially, participants may experience a feeling of vulnerability when they expose their assumptions to others. Over time, this feeling dissipates. The parties share a sense of playfulness with new ideas and develop friendships.

- **A facilitator**—The purpose of having a facilitator is to hold the context of the dialogue and keep the group from the habit of pulling towards discussion. Relatively few people have skills in dialogue, while all of us practice discussion every day. Therefore, while it is easy for us to advocate a position, it is very difficult for us to suspend our assumptions. First, we are often not aware of them, thinking that our positions are the truth rather than a representation of the truth; and second, we can easily revert back to defending our positions since it is our normal form of discourse. A facilitator limits this tendency.

FACILITATING A DIALOGUE: There are different approaches to conducting a dialogue session. A format that is particularly useful for groups that are new to the process is as follows:

FACILITATING AN INTRODUCTORY DIALOGUE SESSION

- Determine if dialogue is appropriate. Is the session's purpose to address complex issues requiring greater collective understanding?

- Designate a facilitator.

- Establish a relaxed atmosphere, where no participants feel rushed.

- If possible, arrange participants in a circle where there are no desks or tables between any two individuals.

- Provide the following guidelines:
    - one person speaks at a time
    - a lapse of time is observed after each person speaks
    - no one comments about another person's remarks
    - participants speak from their own perspective (I think..., My assumption is..., My perspective is...)
    - people are given the opportunity to speak, going sequentially around the room
    - no one is required to speak
    - have a time frame for completion.

- State the topic to be addressed.

- Conduct the dialogue according to the established guidelines.

Once participants are familiar with the process, the formal rules outlined above can be relaxed. At times, particularly with groups that are familiar with dialogue, it may be appropriate for the group leader or facilitator to formally shift between dialogue and discussion within the same session, depending upon the work necessary at any point in time.

DESIRED RESULT: The primary result of an effective dialogue is that collective thoughts go beyond any one individual's understanding, and participants learn together. People become observers of their own assumptions, which they can then hold up to scrutiny. Participants tend to have a richer understanding of complex issues compared to their viewpoint when they entered the conversation. Over time, regular dialogue participants develop deep trust with one another.

As mentioned in the case study, American Woodmark has used formal dialogue sessions as part of its five-day off-site leadership training since its inception in 1993. These sessions have been of particular benefit in helping participants gain a shared sense of purpose and meaning for their respective roles in the company, as well as a grounding in the values and historical roots of the enterprise.

IMPLICATIONS FOR LEADERS

Key points are as follows.

- Since organizations typically use discussion as their primary mode of conversation, leaders should make a conscious effort to consider when the use of dialogue may be more appropriate.

- Dialogue is particularly useful, in conjunction with the 7-Step Process, in creating shared visions and a common understanding of reality.

- Dialogue is also of benefit in discovering mental models, as described in the next chapter.

- Understanding discourse—including how and when to use either discussion or dialogue—is an effective tool that is relatively easy to implement.

SUMMARY

Both discussion and dialogue are beneficial methods of discourse. We can use *discussion* to defend positions and make decisions and *dialogue* to generate new views, create ideas and learn collectively. Effective leadership requires the balancing of discussion and dialogue, depending upon the purpose of the conversation. Understanding the appropriate methods of discourse supports the culture of exceptional organizations by enabling its members to better understand reality, develop new ideas and create more innovative visions.

FUTURE STUDY

- Recall conversations you have had. To what degree were they either discussion or dialogue? Consider whether or not a different mode of conversation would have been more appropriate.

- Meet with a group that will benefit from an interaction using dialogue. Establish a facilitator and follow the procedures described in the example included in the text.

RELATED CHAPTERS

- Essays: "What Do I Want?": 78
            "*Not Knowing* is Your Friend": 89

- Lessons: The 7-Step Process: 183
             Mental Models: 210

30

MENTAL MODELS

This lesson provides an understanding of mental models: what they are, where they come from, why they are important and the nature of their power. It describes how we can hold our mental models up to scrutiny to adopt a new viewpoint.

BACKGROUND

This lesson is based in part upon the work of Peter M. Senge in *The Fifth Discipline*.

THE NATURE OF MENTAL MODELS

We can define "mental models" as our *internal pictures of how the world works*. The creation of mental models is the natural way that we process, organize and give meaning to the data we receive through our senses. Our mental models are important because they not only determine how we make sense of the world but also how we take action. For example, if we believe that people are trustworthy, we act differently than if we believe they are not.

For the thirty year period prior to 2007, existing home prices in America rose every year on average over five percent per year. Looking at the world from this perspective, homeowners held the following mental model.

- Housing prices rise each year.

- Purchasing a home is a riskless investment.

This mental model served homeowners well for a number of years. People borrowed heavily to purchase homes as nice as they could possibly afford and were rewarded by appreciation in their values. But from their peak in 2007, home prices dropped in total more than 25 percent, and many who had significant borrowings on their homes suddenly found that their housing investments had become net liabilities after consideration of their debt obligations.[1] As this example indicates, the quality of our mental models has a tremendous impact upon whether or not our actions will generate desired results.

THE LADDER OF INFERENCE

Where do mental models come from? In *The Fifth Discipline*, Senge states that the process by which we create mental models is the ladder of inference. By inference, he means arriving at a conclusion based upon available evidence. The ladder of inference symbolizes the process of creating mental models by reaching a series of conclusions. Exhibit 30.1 shows each conclusion represented by a rung on the ladder.

OBSERVABLE DATA: At the lowest rung is the full range of *observable data*. This represents all of the sensory information and experiences that come to us; everything we can see, hear, touch, smell and taste. We are continually exposed to huge amounts of information, but we are consciously aware of only a very small fraction of it. For example, as you read this lesson you are most likely unaware of all the background sounds around you, whether they be voices of other people or the hum of a heating or air conditioning system.

SELECTIVE ATTENTION: As we grow from infants to children to adults, we learn to attend to specific data. This is usually information which has the potential to result in either a positive experience or the elimination of a negative one. Because we "select" what to attend to, this process is called *selective attention*, which is the second rung of the ladder. Selective attention allows a sleeping mother to hear her baby cry even though she sleeps through many louder sounds. It also enabled home buyers to attend to the fact that housing prices continued to rise.

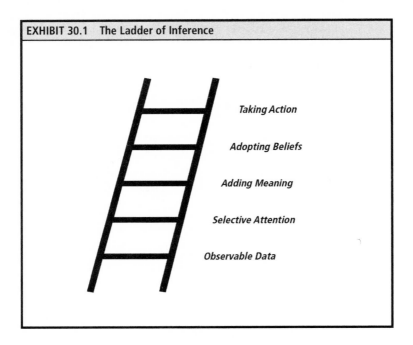

EXHIBIT 30.1   The Ladder of Inference

Taking Action

Adopting Beliefs

Adding Meaning

Selective Attention

Observable Data

ADDING MEANING: The third rung of the ladder is *adding meaning*. Once we have selectively attended to certain data, we add meaning to the information based upon our personal experiences and cultural understanding. The baby's cry means that the baby is in distress. An increase in home prices in the past means that they will continued to rise in the future. The mother and the home buyer both draw upon prior experiences and lessons from our culture. The mother has experienced her baby's cry in the past, and her cultural learning may have included conversations with other mothers. Home buyers observed their friends' homes increase in value over time. All of these experiences and inputs help the mother and the home buyer add meaning to the data they have selected.

ADOPTING BELIEFS: The fourth rung is *adopting beliefs,* or drawing conclusions about the world. Based upon the meaning of what we learn, we generalize our understanding of the specific situation to a belief covering a range of similar situations. The mother adopts the belief that "whenever my baby cries, she needs my help." The home buyer concludes that "home ownership is a riskless investment."

TAKING ACTION: The fifth rung is *taking action* based upon one's beliefs. When people use mental models to evaluate data and make decisions, they "leap" from observable data to action. This is called a *leap of abstraction.* The mother goes to her baby when she cries. Home buyers borrow as much money as possible to acquire the most expensive home they can afford.

Exhibit 30.2 shows the ladder of inference for the mother and for home buyers. Exhibit 30.3 shows the canine version of the ladder of inference.

EXHIBIT 30.2 The Ladder of Inference		
STEP	**MOTHER**	**HOME BUYERS**
Taking Action	Go to baby	Buy the most expensive home one can afford
Adopting Beliefs	When the baby cries, she needs my help	Home ownership is a riskless investment
Adding Meaning	The baby is in distress	Housing prices will not drop
Selective Attention	Baby's cry	Home prices have risen each year
Observable Data	All sounds: TV, heating and air conditioning, wind, voices and baby's cry	People buy homes

EXHIBIT 30.3   Canine Ladder of Inference

THE PROBLEM WITH MENTAL MODELS

Without the ability to create and act upon mental models, it would be impossible for us to survive. Our development from infancy to adulthood entails the continuous learning of more and more mental models which enable us to live in this world.

The problem with mental models lies not in whether they are right or wrong. By their nature all mental models are simplifications, so they can never be completely correct. Problems arise primarily after the models are formed. Once we hold a mental model, we begin to think that our beliefs are the truth and that this truth is obvious. We select data that supports this mental model and disregard other data. We believe the data we select are the "real data" and that our beliefs are based on this real data. Our ability to achieve results is often eroded by this thinking.

Home buyers did not say, "We have a *mental model* that housing prices will continue to rise." They said, "Housing prices will continue to rise." From their perspective, they knew the truth, and since they knew it, they saw no need to question its validity. They did not realize that they only held a *mental* model of reality.

DISCOVERING MENTAL MODELS

If mental models are so difficult to unearth, how do we go about surfacing them? We can do so by holding them up to scrutiny. Senge described three steps to surface, examine and if appropriate change the mental models we hold. These steps are the acts of *reflection, advocacy* and *inquiry*.

REFLECTION: Individual reflection is a first step to surface mental models. We can do so by:

- **Slowing down our thinking**—When we do, we become more aware that we may, in fact, hold a *mental model* of reality and not the *truth* about reality.

- **Asking, "Have we selectively attended to only the data that supports a previously held position?"**—"Do we have other data available that might further support or refute our conclusions?"

- **Asking, "Are the beliefs and conclusions reached appropriate for the data observed?"**—"Are we willing to consider that our mental model is inaccurate?" "Have we substituted overly simple concepts for complex and disparate details?" "Are there alternative conclusions that might be more appropriate?"

- **Asking, "Are the conclusions reached testable?"**—To test the adequacy of our mental models, can we examine different data from that upon which we made our conclusions?"

ADVOCACY: A second step in surfacing mental models is to *advocate* our views to others by:

- **Making our reasoning explicit**—"How did we arrive at our views?" "What is the data we selected, and what are the conclusions reached based upon this data?"

- **Encouraging others to explore our thinking**—"Do they see gaps in our reasoning?"

- **Encourage others to provide different views**—"Do they have different data, alternative conclusions or both?"

- **Inquire if others have views different from our own**—"What are their views?" "How did they arrive at them?"

INQUIRY: The third method for surfacing mental models is to *inquire* about the mental models held by others. By doing so, we better understand not only another's position but also our own. We can do this by:

- **Being genuinely interested in the other's response**—"What are they thinking?"

- **Seeking to clearly understand the other's views**—"What are our assumptions about the other's position?"

- **Asking about the "data" upon which their assumptions are based**—"Do we see how their beliefs are supported by the data they present?"

- **Being willing to consider a position different from our own**—"How reasonable is the other's position?" "Are we willing to reevaluate our own mental models on the subject?"

By practicing reflection, advocacy and inquiry, we explore the limits of our thinking, accept the possibility of being wrong and embrace a willingness to change. By creating an ongoing orientation of holding our mental models up to scrutiny, we learn new ways of understanding the world and adapting our behavior.

PARADIGM SHIFTS

A paradigm is another name for a mental model. A *paradigm shift* occurs when an individual or a group of people shift their thinking from holding one mental model about a specific situation to embracing a radically new picture of the world, one which by its nature is incompatible with the prior belief. As described in his book, *Books That Changed the World*, Robert B. Downes gives the example of one of the most important paradigms in the history of the world.

Today, we all believe that the earth and the other planets which make up our solar system rotate around the sun. Compared to the overall history of humankind, however, this understanding is a relatively new experience. People have forever watched the sun rise in the east and set in the west. From this observation, it was easy to conclude that the sun revolved around the earth.

As mentioned previously, the work of one individual, Nicolaus Copernicus, dispelled this concept. The theory proposed by Copernicus was that the earth was indeed not stationary but rotated on an axis once daily and around the sun once each year. In 1543, he published his findings in his book entitled *De Revolutionibus Orbium Celestrium* (*Concerning the Revolutions of the Heavenly Spheres*).

Although both the presentation of his arguments and the completeness of his supporting physical evidence were powerful, acceptance of the Copernican system was very slow, not only among the general population but also within the scientific community. Most responses were strongly in opposition to the Copernican theories with the most vehement reactions coming from the religious community. The problem with his theories was that, if held, they would upset the established philosophical and religious beliefs of the time. No longer would humankind's home on earth be the center of the universe.

In 1615, the Catholic Church dismissed the Copernican model of the universe in the following statement:

The first proposition, that the sun is the center and does not revolve about the earth, is foolish, absurd, false in theology and heretical, because it is expressly contrary to Holy Scripture. The second proposition, that the earth revolves about the sun and is not the center is absurd, false in philosophy and from a theological point of view at least, opposed to the true faith. [2]

In 1616, the following year, the Church placed the writings of Copernicus on the Index, a listing of books which church members were forbidden to read. A follower of Copernicus, the scientist Giordano Breno, was tried before the Inquisition for blasphemy, was condemned and burned at the stake. In 1633, the famous Italian astronomer, Galileo Galilei, threatened with torture and death by the Inquisition, was compelled on his knees to renounce his beliefs in the Copernican theories. He spent the rest of his life under house arrest.

In spite of the vehement resistance, the Copernican system gradually gained acceptance over the two-hundred-year period following its introduction, as the work of Galileo, John Kepler, Isaac Newton and many others built upon Copernican theories. But not until 1835, almost three hundred years from its first publication, did the work of Copernicus come off the Index. The paradigm shift was complete.

The Copernican concepts were logically presented with sound physical supporting evidence. Why then did it take so long for them to gain acceptance? The term "mental model" may imply that we use rational or logical processes to form and maintain our beliefs, and indeed we do. However, our being at its deepest level—which we describe variously as our emotions, heart, conscience, soul, or simply our gut—acts as a key determinant of this rational process for creating and holding our mental models. We naturally select data and add meaning to that data to generate or reinforce mental models which meet our needs and desires at this most basic level. The Copernican conception of the universe was not simply another scientific advance in astronomy. On the contrary, it threatened people at their very cores—their place in the universe and their relationships with God. If the earth was not the center of the universe, then neither was humankind, and therefore people might no longer be God's most important creation. No wonder resistance was high and acceptance low. What was the evidence that most people selectively attended to? It certainly wasn't the materials published by Copernicus, nor was it the observations of his followers. No, in order to specifically keep the general populace from learning about Copernican concepts, the Church fathers banned the book. Rather than *observe* Galileo's data supporting Copernicus, the Church *selectively attended* to only his recant of Copernicus—"data" extracted through threat of torture. It was only after an overwhelming preponderance of evidence that the pre-Copernican mental model broke down.

The response to Copernicus demonstrates what happens when a new mental model challenges an existing one that has previously met our basic emotional or spiritual needs. A scene from the movie *Lorenzo's Oil* shows the opposite situation, when new data supports a mental model which much better meets one's fundamental desires.

As described in the essay, "Any Luck?," *Lorenzo's Oil* is the true story about a boy, Lorenzo, who in May 1984 was diagnosed as having a rare degenerative brain disease Adrenolenkodystrophy, or ALD. Over a period of years, ALD destroys the protective sheaths around the brain cells eventually causing the loss of all brain function and death. Lorenzo's parents, Augusto and Michaela Odone, were told by doctors that there was no cure for the disease and no hope for Lorenzo. The Odones, however, could not just accept this fate, and so they spearheaded an effort by scientists to come up with "Lorenzo's Oil," a formula which arrested Lorenzo's deteriorating condition but which did not correct any of the previous damage done.

A scene from the movie demonstrates the dramatic paradigm shift that occurred among other parents at an ALD Family Conference in 1987. Prior to this conference, these parents had accepted the prevailing mental model that "there is no hope for my child," and therefore they listened with polite positive acceptance as a researcher Dr. Nickolai, from NIH, described proposed trials or protocols for the eventual development of a therapy for ALD.

As these families listened, they thought that the described therapy, if effective, would benefit future generations of ALD patients but certainly not their own children. However, a woman from the audience interrupted Dr. Nickolai to ask if the new protocol was the result of the success of the therapy with Lorenzo. The doctor responded affirmatively saying that indeed it was and that it was the reason why they were doing the protocol. She then said that the therapy had also worked for her son and that she had gotten the oil from the Odones.

The therapy results for two ALD boys provided new data for the audience—evidence that a therapy was successful on children currently suffering from ALD. Suddenly, the energy level in the room rose dramatically, and people started asking Dr. Nickolai about the availability of this oil. The doctor explained that it was first necessary to conduct a series of protocol trials and then submit the results to the FDA for further review, which everyone realized was a process that would take several years. However, another woman shouted out that AID's patients were given the experimental drug Laetril before all protocols were complete, because the AID's patients were dying anyway.

This woman's comment about Laetril and the knowledge of the two boys' success with the therapy were all the data necessary to spark a dramatic paradigm shift. The parents, who had only moments before listened patiently and appreciatively to Dr. Nickolai, were now on their feet screaming, "I want that oil!" The pressure from these families led to FDA approval of Lorenzo's Oil for use as an experimental drug without the traditional protocol process. Since its development, many ALD children are now able to lead more normal and productive lives.

The paradigm shift at the ALD Conference occurred literally in a matter of minutes. Why did this shift occur so quickly when the Copernican paradigm shift took almost three hundred years? The answer is that the newly created paradigm "there is hope for my child" rather than being a threat helped these parents better meet a most basic need— their love for their children and their deep desire to care for, protect and help them to grow and be healthy. Once they had sufficient data to support the new paradigm, they immediately grasped for it.

We can conclude that it is difficult for us to challenge mental models that we find to be to our disadvantage, particularly those that bring into question the most important beliefs in our lives. To the contrary, it is much easier to adopt a belief that is to our benefit. The more advantageous this belief, the greater is our willingness to adopt it.

The creation of American Woodmark's 1995 Vision, as described in the case study, was the result of a major paradigm shift in my thinking from a mental model that held that providing significant product variety on short lead-times was cost prohibitive to a new belief that providing such variety could be accomplished with minimum cost premiums. As I mentioned, this shift took place in the course of my reading a single business article, or in a matter of minutes.

People in our manufacturing ranks, when they first learned of the 1995 Vision, quickly formed the view that they should resist its implementation to "save the company" by maintaining the status quo. After March 4th 1991, when our two largest home center accounts indicated that they were replacing up to 50 percent of our sales to them, these same people now feared the status quo. They had a sudden paradigm shift, now believing that we needed to implement the

1995 Vision as quickly as possible to again "save the company." Similar to the Odones, our manufacturing people adopted beliefs that they thought were to their own and the organization's best interests. These beliefs were deeply held. It was only through overwhelming evidence that they had a shift in thinking to a new paradigm.

IMPLICATIONS FOR LEADERS

Key points are as follows.

- Leaders must be open to challenging their own mental models and learning the skills to do so.

- Organizations that continually assess the adequacy of their mental models have a significant competitive advantage over those that do not.

- Of particular note to leaders are mental models that are fundamental to the viability and sustainability of the enterprise.

- The greater the willingness to test these mental models, the greater the likelihood that organizations will surface break-through paradigm shifts, which if acted upon will dramatically disrupt traditional structures of the competitive landscape. Such shifts in industry dynamics can lead to quantum changes in organizational effectiveness.

SUMMARY

Mental models are our "internal pictures of how the world works." They are important because they determine not only how we see the world but also how we take action. Mental models are created through the ladder of inference, where we select data, add meaning, adopt a belief and take action.

We can use reflection, advocacy and inquiry to test the adequacy of our mental models. A paradigm shift occurs when we substitute one mental model for another. The more disadvantageous a new belief is to our deepest needs, the more difficult it will be to adopt. On the contrary, we more readily embrace mental models that are to our benefit. The capacity to challenge mental models is critical to the creation and maintenance of exceptional organizations.

FUTURE STUDY

- Look for areas in your professional or personal life where you hold mental models that are different from those held by others. Use "reflection" to examine the adequacy of your beliefs. If possible, meet with these other parties and use "advocacy" and "inquiry" to better understand your beliefs relative to theirs.

- Reflect upon a time when your mental model changed—where you had a paradigm shift. Describe the shift in terms of the ladder of inference for both the prior and the new mental model. How did this change come about?

RELATED CHAPTERS

- Essay: *"Not Knowing* is Your Friend": 89

- Lessons: Culture: 150
             Understanding Discourse: 204

31

HUMAN MOTIVATION

This lesson shows how human motivation impacts behavior. It describes how we can take action to meet our desires, make primary and secondary choices in support of our aspirations and values and create new alternatives when our motivations are in conflict. With this understanding, we can better serve our own and the organization's best interests.

BACKGROUND

This lesson is based in part on the work of Robert Fritz as described in his books, *The Path of Least Resistance* and *The Path of Least Resistance for Managers*.

WHAT MOTIVATES US?

Robert Fritz states that human motivation is the result of a discrepancy between what we want, "our desired state," and what we have, "our current state." This discrepancy creates *tension*, which leads to actions to resolve it. This occurs when the actual state becomes the same as the desired state, as diagrammed in Exhibit 31.1.

Exhibit 31.2 shows a simple example of human motivation. When our desired level of hydration is different from our current state, we get thirsty and drink water until our desired and current level of hydration are one and the same. These relationships create a simple *tension-resolution* system, where being thirsty is the tension and drinking water is the resolution.

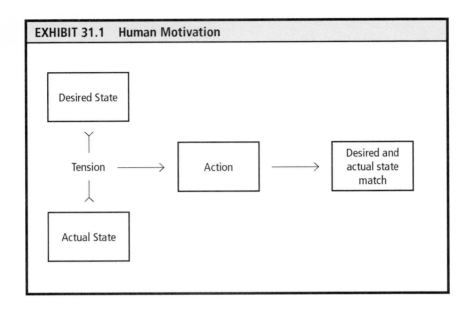

EXHIBIT 31.1   Human Motivation

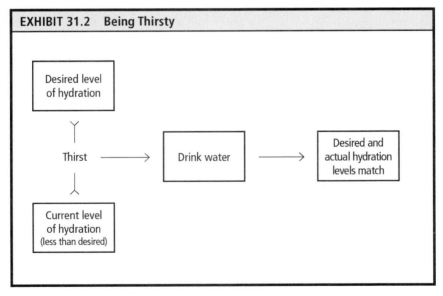

EXHIBIT 31.2   Being Thirsty

Fritz defines the tension between the desired state and the actual state as *structural tension,* as diagrammed in Exhibit 31.3. Structural tension is the basis of all human motivation.

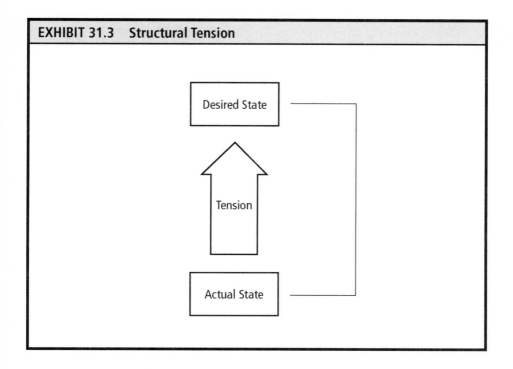

EXHIBIT 31.3   Structural Tension

Desired State

Tension

Actual State

PRIMARY AND SECONDARY CHOICES

Some of our *aspirations*—what we desire—are primary in the sense that we want them for their own sake. Similarly our *core values*—how we want to be—are also primary. When we decide to organize our lives according to our aspirations and values, we make *primary choices* that become concrete, desired end results. We also make *secondary choices* that support the achievement of primary choices. Exhibit 31.4 diagrams these relationships.

We may have a general desire to take care of our children. So, we make a primary choice to provide for their upbringing and education. We make a secondary choice to earn sufficient money to provide for them in the manner we aspire to. Exhibit 31.5 presents an example.

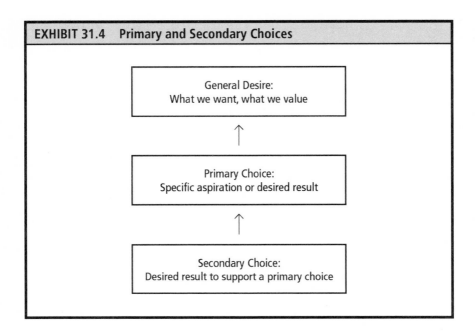

EXHIBIT 31.4   Primary and Secondary Choices

General Desire:
What we want, what we value

Primary Choice:
Specific aspiration or desired result

Secondary Choice:
Desired result to support a primary choice

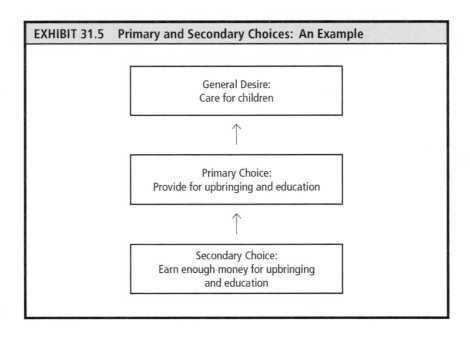

EXHIBIT 31.5   Primary and Secondary Choices: An Example

General Desire:
Care for children

Primary Choice:
Provide for upbringing and education

Secondary Choice:
Earn enough money for upbringing
and education

STRUCTURAL CONFLICT

Conflict occurs when tension-resolution systems compete. Fritz describes a classic example. When we are hungry, we resolve our tension by eating, as shown in Exhibit 31.6. If this were the only system operating, life would be grand. However, if we are overweight, we have a different tension which we resolve by dieting, shown in Exhibit 31.7.

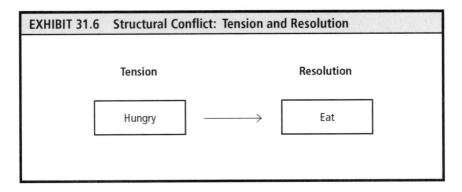

EXHIBIT 31.6   Structural Conflict: Tension and Resolution

Tension   Resolution

Hungry   ⟶   Eat

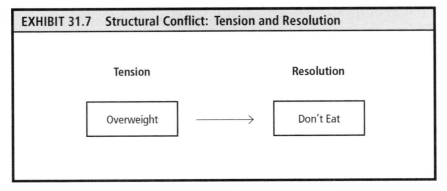

EXHIBIT 31.7   Structural Conflict: Tension and Resolution

Tension   Resolution

Overweight   ⟶   Don't Eat

The two tension-resolution systems are related and in conflict. We cannot resolve both tensions at the same time—we cannot simultaneously "eat" and "not eat." Exhibit 31.8 structures this conflict.

When we eat, we reduce the tension on the hungry-eat system (arrow 1). Not only are we satiated, but we also gain weight and increase the tension on the overweight—don't-eat system (arrow 2). The path of least resistance is now to reduce this tension by dieting (arrow 3). But once we have stopped eating and lose weight, we become hungry again, and the tension now increases with the hungry—eat system (arrow 4). People who diet, lose weight and then gain it back are acting within this structure.

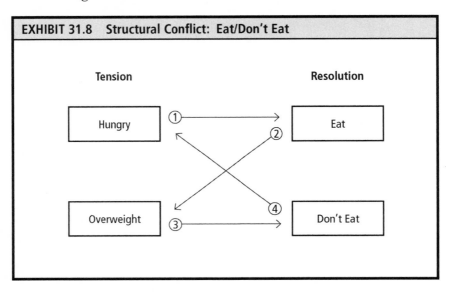

EXHIBIT 31.8   Structural Conflict: Eat/Don't Eat

Fritz defines *structural conflict* as two or more tension-resolution systems in which the points of resolution are mutually exclusive. It is natural to attempt to resolve a structural conflict. However, these efforts will not work because there can be no final resolution, only oscillation or movement back and forth between mutually exclusive points. When we are on a swing, we cannot simultaneously be at both the highest point in front of the swing and at the highest point in back of it. Once we reach one high point, all of the momentum is gone and the potential energy caused by gravity takes us back to the other high point. It is only by changing the underlying structure that we can make any real changes to take us to a new place.

Although we cannot resolve a structural conflict, we can create a structural-tension system that is senior to it and which takes precedence over it. When this occurs, our existing structural conflict becomes part of our current reality. We may still continue to oscillate between mutually exclusive points, but this conflict will recede in importance as we move toward the resolution of a senior structure which is dominant. If our structural conflict between eating and dieting is the only structure in effect, we will continue to oscillate between these two behaviors. If, however, we make a primary choice to be healthy, then we create a more senior structure—one of structural tension, as shown in Exhibit 31.9.

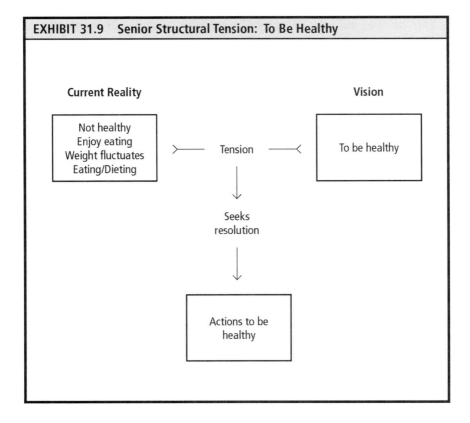

EXHIBIT 31.9   Senior Structural Tension: To Be Healthy

Current Reality

Vision

Not healthy
Enjoy eating
Weight fluctuates
Eating/Dieting

Tension

To be healthy

Seeks
resolution

Actions to be
healthy

The tension created by the disparity between the vision to be healthy and the current reality of not being healthy may lead to a number of actions to improve health: exercise, getting a physical examination, relaxation, taking vitamins—in addition to altering eating patterns. The conflict of "eat—don't-eat" may still exist, but it may recede in importance. Having our "favorite dessert" may become less important than improving and maintaining health. Weight might still fluctuate but around a narrower range that is considerably healthier. The conflict is still there, but it doesn't matter as much relative to the primary choice to be healthy.

CONFLICTING VALUES

Our values guide our behavior—whether we are trustworthy, compassionate, truthful, loyal or courageous. Sometimes, however, our values come into conflict, and we have to choose an action that will simultaneously support one value but betray another. For example, we may value "honesty" and "loyalty" when giving an employment reference for a former coworker for whom we have had job performance concerns. Should we be totally honest or completely loyal? Although we may vacillate about what to do, once we do take action, our behavior may be more in accordance with one value than another. It is when we face such a conflict that our predominant values are revealed.

OBSERVATIONS ON MOTIVATIONS

We often witness different human motivations.

- When Sam's job is going well, he wants recognition and rewards.

- When an economic downturn threatens his organization, Sam wants security to keep his job and provide for his family.

- Betty values the organization's mission and is passionate about helping the organization achieve its vision. She organizes her work-life to support this priority. She is not particularly motivated by recognition, rewards or job security.

- Bob oscillates between taking on more challenging responsibilities which he would enjoy and staying in his existing position where he is more comfortable.

We can make several observations about what we have learned.

- We want what we want, and we value what we value. We can't will ourselves nor can others will us to want something we don't want or value what we don't value.

- What motivates one person does not necessarily motivate another.

- If circumstances change, what we want may change.

- A met desire is no longer a source of motivation.

- A met need may not stay met and therefore may become a new desire.

- Behaviors may oscillate because multiple motivations that cannot be simultaneously met.

- When values are in conflict, our actions will reflect which ones dominate.

- We can organize our lives around our aspirations and values, making secondary choices to support them.

IMPLICATIONS FOR LEADERS

An understanding of human motivation has several implications.

- Since organizations cannot impose values on individuals, it is important that we hire and advance people who have values that match those which our organizations' embrace.

- We can inspire people by presenting them with opportunities which are consistent with their own values and aspirations.

- Being sensitive to what motivates particular individuals in specific circumstances is critical to leading them in their own and the organization's best interests.

- Although we can't will a particular motivation or determine a particular behavior, leaders can create environments—such as with rewards and punishments—which can influence behavior because the environment satisfies already established motivations.

- There is no formula—each individual and each circumstance is unique.

- Understanding human motivation is a key skill for leaders who are intent on creating exceptional organizations.

SUMMARY

This lesson provides a basic understanding of human motivation and its implications for organizations and their leaders. We make primary and secondary choices to support our aspirations and values. Our behaviors may oscillate because we have a structural conflict between competing structural-tension systems. By understanding human motivation, we can better lead individuals for both their organizations' and their own benefit.

FUTURE STUDY

- Think of some of your recent behaviors. Describe them as tension-resolution systems. For each, indicate the discrepancy between the desired state and the actual state.

- Describe a general aspiration or value you have and any primary and secondary choices you have made to support it.

- Diagram, as shown in the lesson, a structural conflict you have experienced.

RELATED CHAPTERS

- Essay: "What Do I Want?": 78

- Lessons: The 7-Step Process: 183
             Ethical Dilemmas: 268

32

WORKING IN TEAMS

This lesson presents the principles of working in teams. It describes when a group becomes a team and shows both the benefits and costs for individuals in joining one. It emphasizes the importance of highly-effective teams to the creation of exceptional organizations, and it presents two types of teams, each of which is critical for doing the work of the enterprise.

BACKGROUND

This lesson is based in part on the unpublished works of Kent Guichard and Roger Vandenberg.

DEFINITION

We can describe an *organization* as "two or more people who come together for a common purpose." In their book, *The Wisdom of Teams,*" Jon Katzenbach and Douglas Smith define a team as "a small group of people with complementary skills who are committed to a common purpose, performance goals and approach for which they hold themselves mutually accountable."[1] With this definition, a team is an "organization" with unique attributes.

WHEN A GROUP BECOMES A TEAM

A group of people is not a team. It becomes one only as the team develops certain attributes, and its members adopt specific behaviors.

TEAM ATTRIBUTES:

- a shared purpose and vision

- an identity beyond the separate identities of the individuals

- recognized roles, hierarchy and leaders

- familiarity among members

- shared history and experiences

- necessary processes

- open communication.

TEAM MEMBER BEHAVIORS:

- *commitment*—holding themselves and others accountable for desired results and making individual sacrifices for the good of the whole

- *trust*—being confident other team members will do what is expected, valuing their contributions and accepting their differences

- *caring*—valuing team members as human beings, caring about their personal growth and development.

With this description, the transition from a group to a team is a gradual evolution as the group takes on more of the characteristics of a team. Even though many of the team attributes may be in place, highly-effective teams do not come into being until team members behave with a heightened sense of *commitment*, *trust* and *caring*.

BENEFITS AND COSTS OF JOINING A TEAM

There are several benefits for individuals in joining a team.

BENEFITS:

- two or more accomplishing what one cannot

- opportunities for individual learning and growth

- camaraderie that builds confidence and provides a support network

- a sense of security in being part of the team

- a sharing in the success of the team.

COSTS:

- teams take time

- changes in individual behavior may be required

- privacy may be foregone

- less individual recognition

- potential vulnerability in front of others

- taking on everyone's burdens

- sharing in the team's failures.

Although it is important to be aware of the costs, individuals who work in teams typically gain great satisfaction and personal growth by being members.

THE IMPORTANCE OF TEAMS FOR ORGANIZATIONS

While a few jobs in organizations may require solely individual effort, most tasks require the effective interaction and participation of two or more people. Structuring work so that it can be accomplished in small teams—ranging from two to twenty but ideally from five to ten—creates the potential for superior results. This potential is released as groups become teams, and teams become highly-effective—with heightened levels of commitment, trust and caring.

There are two categories of teams within organizations—*natural-work teams* and *cross-functional teams.*

NATURAL-WORK TEAMS: The purpose of natural-work teams is to more effectively accomplish tasks that involve people who normally work together. They are comprised of supervisors and those reporting directly to them. They have the following characteristics.

NATURAL-WORK TEAM CHARACTERISTICS

- They are organized according to the traditional management hierarchy.

- Supervisors are team leaders, and their direct reports are team members.

- Supervisors retain their hierarchical authority.

- Teams have common goals and measures of performance.

- All team members are responsible for goal achievement.

- Team members share in the success of the team.

CROSS-FUNCTIONAL TEAMS: The purpose of cross-functional teams is to better accomplish tasks that require the involvement of people from separate functional areas. They are comprised of a designated team leader and team members from different parts of the organization, all of whom have additional job responsibilities independent of those of the team. They are characterized as follows.

CROSS-FUNCTIONAL TEAM CHARACTERISTICS

- A member of senior management, who has the authority to act on behalf of the organization, acts as the team sponsor.

- The sponsor chooses the team leader.

- The team's leader chooses its members with the approval of the team member's supervisor.

- The sponsor issues a *charge statement* to the team designating its purpose, resources available and constraints.

- Once the team's purpose is achieved, the team is disbanded.

- Some cross-functional teams may be on-going as long as they serve an ongoing purpose of the organization.

Natural-work teams and cross-functional teams are the fundamental structures by which exceptional organizations do the work necessary to achieve their goals.

As described in the case study and the essay, "A Bad Plan Poorly Executed," American Woodmark's ability to work with natural-work teams and cross-function teams was a fundamental building block for the achievement of our 1995 Vision. Although simple in concept, we went through a number of trials and errors before we successfully created this capacity.

IMPLICATIONS FOR LEADERS

Leaders can utilize the following checklist to effectively utilize teams in their organizations.

1. Establish whether the work to be done should be done by an individual, a natural-work team or a cross-functional team.

2. Assure that the team is comprised of people who have the necessary skills to achieve the task.

3. Establish ground rules to guide behaviors.

4. Create a vision of the team's desired results.

5. Gain *commitment* by helping team members create a shared acceptance of the vision and establish mutual accountability.

6. Gain a shared understanding of current reality relative to the vision.

7. Take action to move the current reality toward the vision.

8. Establish *trust* among team members as each individual makes their respective contributions to the team's efforts and learns to accept other team members' differences.

9. Promote *caring* among team members by creating time apart from task-related activities to interact socially and learn about each others' backgrounds, family, interests and aspirations.

10. Resolve unacceptable behaviors that might impact the achievement of the team's vision, the individuals' responsibilities to the team and other team members and adherence to the team's ground rules.

11. Celebrate the achievement of milestones and final results.

By using this checklist to create visions for their teams, leaders dramatically increase the likelihood that their team members will look beyond their own self-interests to be *inspired* to help achieve the organization's purpose and highest aspirations.

SUMMARY

Individuals who work in effective teams typically gain great satisfaction and personal growth by being members. Teams play a significant role in helping organizations achieve their purposes. Highly-effective teams—those that engender a heightened level of *commitment, trust* and *caring* among members—are fundamental building blocks to the creation of exceptional organizations.

FUTURE STUDY

- Evaluate the effectiveness of teams you have participated in relative to the principles in this lesson.

- If you are leading a team, use the "Checklist for Team Leaders" as a guide.

RELATED CHAPTER

- Essay: A Bad Plan Poorly Executed: 110

THE JOURNEY

This section presents three lessons that address some of the issues that arise along the journey toward creating exceptional organizations. The first, "Working in Alignment," describes how to measure performance and modify actions as necessary in the pursuit of this goal. The second, "Cultural Change," shows the barriers to organizational change and the steps to be taken to overcome them. The third, "Ethical Dilemmas," provides a method for living according to one's core values by offering a technique for resolving right-versus-right choices where one value is in conflict with another.

33

WORKING IN ALIGNMENT

This lesson describes how to organize work to achieve the goals of the enterprise. It shows how to measure performance and modify actions as necessary to achieve the desired results.

BACKGROUND

This material is based in part upon the work of Robert Fritz in his book, *The Path of Least Resistance for Managers*.

WORK HIERARCHY

We can define the *work* of an organization as the "actions taken in pursuit of its purpose." Work is *what* an organization does. *Working in alignment* means that actions are orchestrated in harmony with one another and are effective and efficient with a minimum of wasted effort.

The lesson, "The 7-Step Process," presented a primary tool for doing work:

THE 7-STEP PROCESS

1. Create a Vision

2. Understand Current Reality

3. Take Action

4. Measure Performance

5. Modify Actions

6. Achieve Results

7. Create a New Vision

Exhibit 33.1 again depicts these steps:

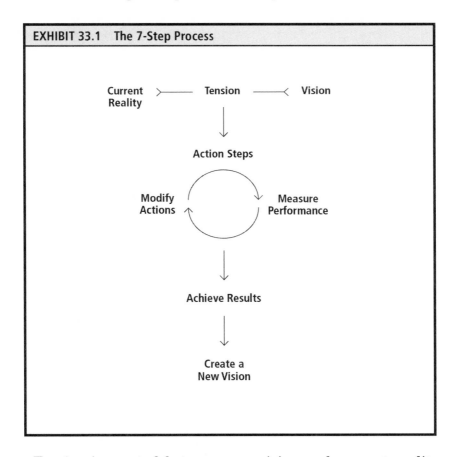

EXHIBIT 33.1   The 7-Step Process

Tension is created between our vision and current reality which leads to our taking action to relieve the tension and move toward our vision. We measure our performance and modify our actions until we achieve our desired results. We then create a new vision.

We can use the 7-Step Process to form a *work hierarchy* as previously described in the Lesson, "Vision-Driven Organizations," to structure work at each level of the organization. Exhibit 33.2 again shows this structure.

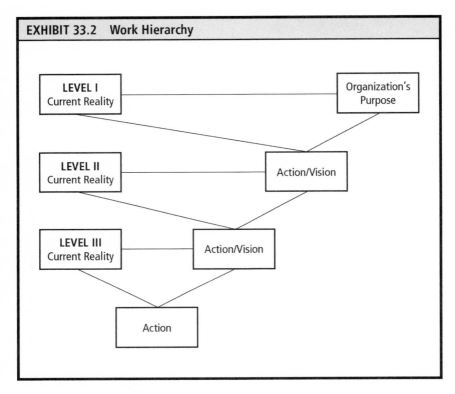

EXHIBIT 33.2   Work Hierarchy

As the example in Exhibit 33.3 shows, the entity's purpose at the corporate level is to provide a service to a particular constituency. Its action is to provide five programs by next January. The *action step* at the corporate level becomes the *vision* at the division level—"Have five programs by next January." Action Step 2—at the division level is to, "Complete Program B by next January." Accomplishing this becomes the vision at the department level, which has several steps for its achievement.

EXHIBIT 33.3   Work Hierarchy: An Example

LEVEL 1 - CORPORATE

- Vision .... Providing a service to a particular constituency
- Current Reality .... Current status relative to this vision
- Action .... Provide five programs by next January

---

LEVEL 2 - DIVISION I

- Vision .... Have five programs by next January
- Current Reality .... Current status relative to this vision
- Action Step 2 (of 5) .... Complete Program B by next January

---

LEVEL 3 - DEPARTMENT II

- Vision .... Have Program B in place by next January
- Current Reality .... Current status relative to this vision
- Action Step 3 (of 6) .... Establish a preliminary design of Program B by June

---

Organizing work on a level-to-level basis assures that all actions necessary to achieve the organization's purpose are clearly established. Furthermore, any activities previously done by the organization, but which are not included in the work hierarchy are identified as being non-essential or wasteful. Working in alignment means that all the necessary, and only the necessary, actions to achieve a vision are done at the right level by the right people at the right time.

MEASURING PERFORMANCE

To maintain alignment, we need to *measure performance* to assure that the actions we take are successful. The question arises, "What is the right data to measure?" There are three categories of data; those which:

- reflect movement toward a vision

- meet expectations of achievement

- influence future actions.

An example of data reflecting *movement toward a vision* is the weekly measurement of on-the-job accidents as part of a safety improvement program. Data that *meets expectations of achievement* would be exemplified by an entity that defines its vision of financial viability as achieving a certain annual cash flow and, therefore, measures its cash flow performance relative to this target. Data to *influence future actions* is exemplified by the use of market research to test the effectiveness of alternative sales promotions.

Other examples of measurements are:

- quarterly or annual financial reports

- performance reviews for employees

- client feedback

- quality audits

- employee surveys.

One particular measurement for organizations is a *scorecard*, which defines a range of goals that must be achieved jointly to achieve success. Exhibit 33.4 shows an example of a department within an organization that provides a product or service. It is responsible for generating a desired output within a specific quality standard, delivery time and cost. Goals for performance criteria are listed along the right side of the card, and actual performance is portrayed across the card for each time period.

| EXHIBIT 33.4 Scorecard |

MEASURE	PERIOD						GOAL
	1	2	3	4	5	6	
Output (Units)	1200	1250	1300	1320			1300
Quality (%)	99	98	97	99			98
On-time Delivery (%)	80	84	92	92			96
Cost ($)	3.80	3.50	3.05	3.05			3.10

RESPONSE TO MEASUREMENTS

Our feelings will differ depending upon whether or not our actions are successful. If they are, we are likely to feel satisfied, happy and energized with a sense of accomplishment. If they are unsuccessful, we may feel disappointed, stressed and frustrated with a sense of failure. No one likes to fail, but we can ask ourselves, "Is failure okay within an organization?" The answer is:

- *yes*—when a legitimate effort is made toward a goal, and the party learns from the experience

- *no*—when the party makes no effort toward the goal, has been negligent, has acted grossly in conflict with the organization's values, or has continuously failed with no prospect for improvement.

Everyone fails at one time or another. In his career, Babe Ruth hit a tremendous number of home runs, but he also struck out a lot. The challenge is to not let individual failures keep us from pursuing our goals. As Henry Ford put it, "Failure is only the opportunity to more intelligently begin again."

MODIFYING ACTIONS

When performance measurements indicate that behaviors are not successful, it is necessary to *modify actions*. The decision to do so may seem straightforward—our actions either work or they don't. However, in reality this decision is much more complex. An example many of us have experienced is getting lost while driving our cars. How many of us have just kept on driving long after we were aware that we didn't have a clue as to where we were? There are many barriers to changing behavior. Some of these are:

- inadequate information on progress

- difficulty in understanding why goals were not achieved

- unwillingness to admit to ourselves and others that our actions were wrong

- fear of change

- a feeling of comfort with past habits and behaviors

- fear of not having the knowledge or skill to go in a new direction

- being uncommitted to the goals in the first place

- a feeling that changing behavior may be an admission of failure

- organizational resistance to change—momentum to proceed as planned.

To facilitate its ability to modify actions, the organization can create an environment that provides a willingness to:

- question existing assumptions

- make major changes when necessary

- set difficult goals, accept risk and expect a certain amount of failure.

With such an environment, failure can become a stepping stone to success.

AMERICAN WOODMARK'S EXPERIENCE

American Woodmark's ability to work in alignment evolved over a number of years. During the 1980s, most of our performance measurement systems were subjective, if they existed at all. For example, quality control was based upon reactions to complaints from customers. There was no accountability for quality because there were no standards upon which to make an evaluation and no way to determine whose actions might have led to a specific result. As part of our 1995 Vision, we began a gradual process that continues to this day of creating measurement systems for critical functions such as production, cost, quality, safety, customer service, delivery, product development and employee performance. We organized work according to work hierarchies with each functional area having its own scorecard measuring its effectiveness. Where the company's ability to work in alignment was a strategic deficiency in the 1980s, it became a source of competitive advantage in the 1990s.

IMPLICATIONS FOR LEADERS

Key points are as follows.

- Many organizations' actions are disconnected from their visions and aspirations. They engage in some activities that are unnecessary, while neglecting others that may be critical for success.

- By organizing action steps into a work hierarchy, leaders can achieve their organizations' goals with the most effective and efficient use of time, money and other resources.

- Leaders need to create cultures that both foster candid appraisals of performance and a willingness to modify actions as soon as appropriate.

- *Working in alignment* is a critical element in the creation of exceptional organizations.

SUMMARY

This lesson provides a methodology to keep the work of the organization in alignment. The basic framework for doing so is the creation of a work hierarchy based upon the principles of the 7-Step Process. To stay in alignment, the organization needs appropriate performance measurements so that actions which are not on track can be modified. When the organization works in alignment, it increases its capability to achieve its purpose and to do so as effectively and efficiently as possible.

FUTURE STUDY

- Think of an organizational project, either actual or imagined, that requires the work of people at multiple levels of the enterprise. Organize the work using the work hierarchy. Include due dates and individuals or departments responsible for the achievement of action steps. Once this is done, establish appropriate performance measures to monitor progress toward the desired result.

- Are there times when you have resisted making a necessary change? If so, what were the barriers to your taking action?

RELATED CHAPTERS

34

CULTURAL CHANGE

This lesson uses systems thinking as a framework for understanding the nature of cultures and, where they are deficient, how to change them.

THE WIDGET DEPARTMENT

Imagine an organization with many departments, one of which produces widgets. The Widget Department is comprised of a supervisor and several workers, all of whom have worked in their current jobs for many years.

The existing production process requires each worker to perform a separate and unique job for the completion of each widget. One day, senior management decides that the organization would benefit from a change in the process, whereby all workers learn each others jobs and rotate through the various work stations. A recently recruited staff person from the corporate office comes to the Widget Department to proudly explain the advantages of the new program for both the organization and the department's workers, who would now learn new skills, be more productive, have more variety in their work and receive a higher wage. Guess the reaction of the workers to this plan—excitement about the new work structure, glad about the pay increase or thankful for the opportunity? A few respond this way. However, most react with *fear*! For these individuals, any good thoughts about the plan are immediately overwhelmed by a concern that they might be unable to meet the new job requirements, putting their jobs in jeopardy.

The department begins the implementation of the new plan under the guidance of the corporate staff person. While there are both positive and negative aspects to the methods used to introduce the plan, can you imagine what the workers focus upon? Those holding a mental model of "fear of job loss" selectively attend to every instance where the program looks flawed. They generalize that the program is no good, and they reject it and offer resistance in any way they can. Eventually the program fails. Senior management gives up on its plan, the staff person returns to the corporate office and work returns to the previous routine with each person working in the same job in the same place. Exhibit 34.1 shows this sequence of events.

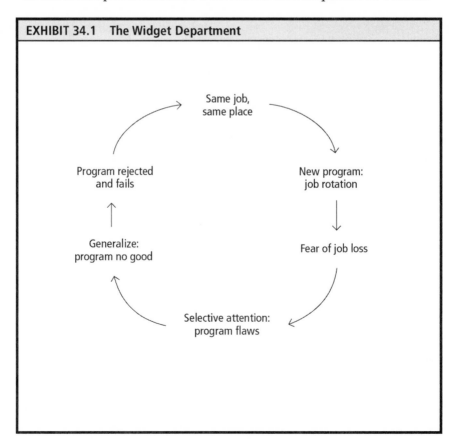

EXHIBIT 34.1   The Widget Department

Same job, same place

New program: job rotation

Fear of job loss

Selective attention: program flaws

Generalize: program no good

Program rejected and fails

If you were the staff person, how would you go about changing the Widget Department to achieve senior management's desired result? Write down your thoughts, and we will return to them later.

SYSTEMS THINKING

Systems thinking provides a framework for understanding cultures. It postulates that all things are interconnected, and that they are interconnected by *systems*. A system is defined as "a collection of parts which interact with each other to function as a whole." All systems are comprised of feedback loops which provide feedback to the system's current state causing it, in the case of *reinforcing loops,* to change its status and move toward a new state and, in the case of *balancing loops,* to maintain the current status setting limits on change.

REINFORCING LOOPS: With reinforcing loops, small changes, if unchecked, lead to exponential growth or contraction. Imagine that you were given one penny on day one, two pennies on day two, four pennies on day three, eight pennies on day four and so on for thirty days. How much money would you have on day 15?—over $163. How much on day 30?—over $5 million. The action of doubling the number of pennies each day creates exponential growth and a change in the status of the number of pennies received each day as presented in Exhibit 34.2. A loop that leads to exponential growth, as in this example, is a *positive reinforcing loop.*

Alternatively, consider a pond that is completely covered with a total of one million lilies. After the first frost in the fall, one half of the lilies die each day. When is the pond half full?—the second day with 500,000 lilies. How many lilies are left after the tenth day?—1,953 lilies. In how many days will it take for there to be one lily remaining in the pond? As shown in Exhibit 34.3, it takes only 21 days.

EXHIBIT 34.2	Pennies Received Each Day		
DAY	PENNIES	DAY	PENNIES
1	1	16	32,768
2	2	17	65,536
3	4	18	131,072
4	8	19	262,144
5	16	20	524,288
6	32	21	1,048,576
7	64	22	2,097,152
8	128	23	4,194,304
9	256	24	8,388,608
10	512	25	16,777,216
11	1,024	26	33,554,432
12	2,048	27	67,108,864
13	4,096	28	134,217,728
14	8,192	29	268,435,456
15	16,384	30	536,870,912

A loop that leads to contraction, as with the case with the lilies, is a *negative reinforcing loop.*

Reinforcing loops have an action, either for growth or contraction that changes the existing status or *condition* as shown in Exhibit 34.4.

In the example of the pennies, the condition is "the number of pennies" at any point in time, and the *growing action* is the "two times increase." In the pond, the condition is "the number of lilies," and the *contracting action* is a "50 percent reduction."

EXHIBIT 34.3   Lillies Remaining Each Day

DAY	LILLIES	DAY	LILLIES
1	1,000,000	12	488
2	500,000	13	244
3	250,000	14	122
4	125,000	15	61
5	62,500	16	31
6	31,250	17	15
7	15,625	18	8
8	7,813	19	4
9	3,906	20	2
10	1,953	21	1
11	977		

EXHIBIT 34.4   Reinforcing Loop

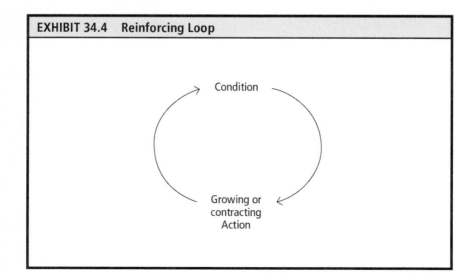

BALANCING LOOPS: With balancing loops, attempts to change the current condition are countered resulting in a return to the initial condition. The greater the attempted change, the more severe the counter measure. Picture that you are driving a car. You start by putting your foot on the accelerator, and the car begins to move. As you keep your foot on the pedal, you go faster until you reach a target or limit which causes you to reduce the pressure. Once you do, the car slows down below the target—perhaps the speed limit—until you eventually accelerate the car again. The system balances around this target, as is illustrated in Exhibit 34.5.

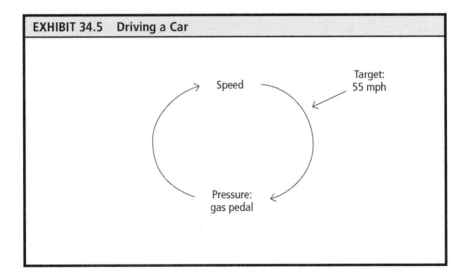

EXHIBIT 34.5   Driving a Car

Balancing loops are tied to a target such as an external goal or constraint. This is illustrated in Exhibit 34.6. In the example of driving a car, the condition is "the speed" at any point in time, the *corrective action* is "pressure on the gas pedal," and the target is "55 miles per hour." It is corrective in that pressure is increased if the current speed is below the target and decreased if it is above the target.

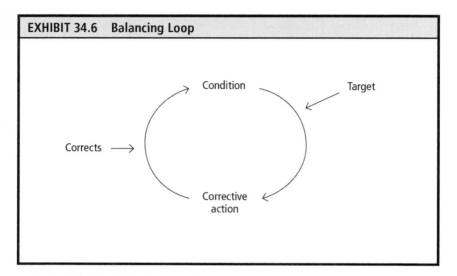

EXHIBIT 34.6   Balancing Loop

INTERCONNECTED SYSTEMS: In our world, individual systems very often combine into larger more complex *interconnected systems*. An example is the relationship between national employment and consumer spending as illustrated in Exhibit 34.7. As consumer spending rises, employment increases, which results in consumer spending rising again, and employment going up again. This is a positive feedback loop. Alternatively, if for some reason consumer spending were to go down, then employment would go down further reducing spending which would further reduce employment. The same relationship can be either positive or negative depending upon whether the initial action is growing or contracting.

This example is a *reinforcing system* because it is characterized by *change*. Once employment and consumer spending start changing, there is nothing within the system to keep them both from either growing to infinity or dropping to zero. In reality, this doesn't happen. The reason is that this reinforcing system continues unchecked only until it reaches a limiting balancing system that acts as a constraint.

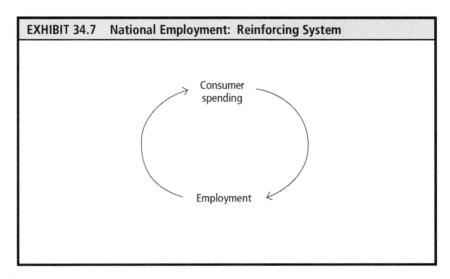

EXHIBIT 34.7   National Employment: Reinforcing System

Consumer spending

Employment

If employment drops below an acceptable level, as measured by the unemployment rate, the government acts to stimulate the economy which then causes employers to invest in their businesses thereby creating new jobs. This continues until the employment level rises to within the targeted level which, when accomplished, results in a reduction of the stimulus, as shown in Exhibit 34.8.

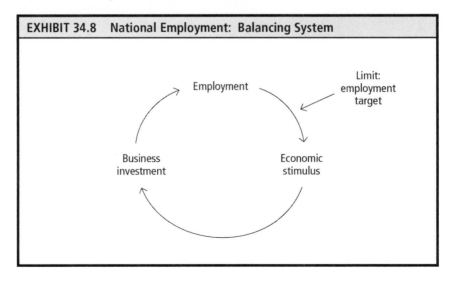

EXHIBIT 34.8   National Employment: Balancing System

Employment

Limit: employment target

Business investment

Economic stimulus

This is a *balancing system* because it is characterized by a balancing loop that keeps the system *stable*. The two systems can be combined into a larger system as shown in Exhibit 34.9 that incorporates the elements of employment, consumer spending, business investment and economic stimulus into an overall economic system.

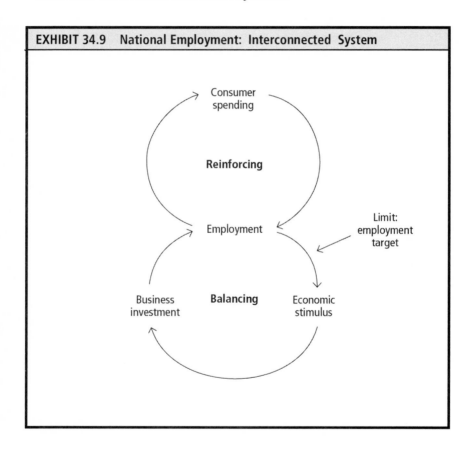

EXHIBIT 34.9   National Employment: Interconnected System

This is an *interconnected system* because it is comprised of separate individual systems. It can be characterized as a balancing system because it will tend to keep employment levels *stable* within a targeted range.

CULTURES AS SYSTEMS

As previously described, an organization's culture consists of its values, beliefs, traditions and processes that guide behavior. A culture is a system in that it has "interconnected parts that function together as a whole." It is a balancing system because it tends to keep its status or condition stable within established parameters. When we say that an organization has a culture, we mean that behaviors tend to remain constant even though the environment changes.

CULTURAL CHANGE

If cultures are, by their nature, stable, how do we change them? To begin, we can use the 7-Step Process to articulate our desired new culture. We can then describe our existing culture in relationship to this vision. The discrepancy between our desired culture and our current status creates tension, which we resolve by taking action to move the existing culture toward our vision.

From a systems-thinking perspective, there are two categories of action steps; first, the creation of reinforcing loops which reinforce movement toward a desired new culture and second, the elimination of balancing loops which keep the culture in its current state. This process is illustrated in Exhibit 34.10.

Let's examine the Widget Department with regard to what we have learned. There is a desire for a new culture incorporating job rotation. The department is a stable system in that it resists attempts to change it. Now, look at the list of actions you previously prepared to change the Widget Department. Which of these would you characterize as steps reinforcing movement toward the desired culture? Which would you describe as eliminating balancing loops keeping the department in its current status?

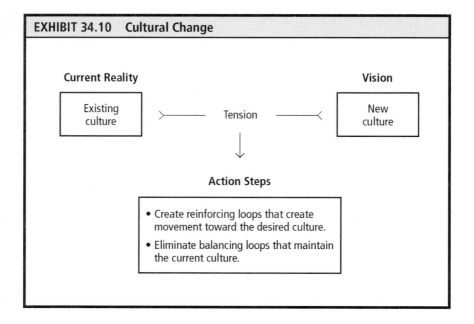

EXHIBIT 34.10   Cultural Change

Current Reality   **Vision**

Existing culture   >—— Tension ——< New culture

Action Steps

- Create reinforcing loops that create movement toward the desired culture.
- Eliminate balancing loops that maintain the current culture.

If your list is typical, your actions will be predominately based upon steps with reinforcing loops to get you to the desired state rather than actions to eliminate balancing loops that keep you where you are. Examples of possible actions for the Widget Department are:

- actions with reinforcing loops:
  - explain benefits of job rotation
  - offer a financial incentive
  - provide adequate training

- actions which eliminate balancing loops:
  - let those with the greatest concerns be the last to convert
  - offer job protection for an extended period
  - provide even more than the perceived adequate training to better help those with the greatest concerns.

It would seem that steps with reinforcing loops that explain the benefits, offer an incentive and provide adequate training would be sufficient to implement the program. However, action steps that eliminate balancing loops such as those that reduce the fear associated with the new program are likely to be critical. Some action steps, such as training, may serve both as a reinforcing step and as the removal of a balancing loop.

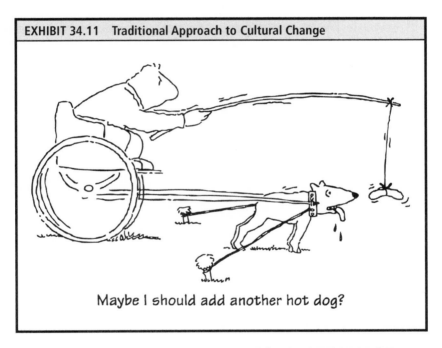

EXHIBIT 34.11   Traditional Approach to Cultural Change

Maybe I should add another hot dog?

AMERICAN WOODMARK'S EXPERIENCE

There were two elements to American Woodmark's 1995 Vision initiated in 1989; first, a substantially new strategy and second, a new culture to support this strategy. The case study and the essays describe some of the steps we took to change our culture. A few points are relevant. First, with my confidence and optimism about our new direction, my initial tendency, similar to the driver in the cartoon above, was to focus on the positive aspects of our change effort. I paid less attention to the barriers that kept the organization from endorsing this change. Second, our corporate culture was extremely complex having evolved over many years. Unfortunately, it did not come with a user's manual. Therefore, it was impossible to know all the answers before proceeding, and we could only learn what to do by trial and error. Third, our cultural change was chaotic. Because we were attempting such a dramatic change, our existing culture—which by its nature was stable—countered our efforts by offering tremendous resistance to maintain the status quo. This resulted in almost universal resistance to all initiatives, making it difficult to determine whether a particular direction was appropriate or not. As a consequence, it often took us longer than one would expect to understand when we had gone in the wrong direction. Our eventual success in changing the culture was the result of our senior team's perseverance in holding our vision, while being open to modifying actions in its pursuit.

IMPLICATIONS FOR LEADERS

Leaders can use the following checklist to create the cultures they desire.

1. Assess whether the existing culture supports the organization's purpose, aspirations and values.

2. If it does, maintain this culture by consciously taking action to preserve it.

3. If the existing culture is inadequate, create a shared vision of the desired culture among key stakeholders.

4. Understand the current reality of the existing culture, including those elements which act as barriers to changing it.

5. Create action steps to change the culture to the desired state. Action steps can include both steps that reinforce movement toward the desired cul-

ture and steps that remove constraints that keep the existing culture in place.

6. Measure the results of the actions taken and modify them as necessary.

7. Once the organization has an exceptional culture— one that supports its purpose, aspirations and values, be vigilant in maintaining its status.

SUMMARY

Cultures are stable systems in that they tend to maintain behavior even though the environment changes. This feature is valuable provided that the existing culture is adequate for the achievement of the organization's purpose. When it isn't, the principles of systems thinking can be used to create a new culture. Using them requires not only taking actions that foster movement toward a new culture, but also steps that eliminate factors that keep the existing culture stable.

FUTURE STUDY

● Make a list of three systems that have either positive or negative reinforcing loops and a second list of three that have balancing loops.

● If you have ever been associated with an organization going through a cultural change, describe the efforts to implement the change from a systems-thinking perspective.

RELATED CHAPTERS

● Essay: Guidance from Gandhi: 107

● Lessons: Culture: 150
          The 7-Step Process: 183
          Mental Models: 210

35

ETHICAL DILEMMAS

This lesson shows how individuals and organizations can make choices when faced with ethical dilemmas, where acting according to one value is in conflict with acting according to another. It describes the characteristics of ethical dilemmas and methods to resolve them. The use of these techniques will support the creation of exceptional organizations.

BACKGROUND

This material is based upon the work of Rushworth M. Kidder in his book, *How Good People Make Tough Choices*.

RIGHT-VERSUS-WRONG CHOICES

How do we make *right versus wrong* choices? The world is full of wrong-doing. Kidder describes three ways to think of it:

- *violation of the law*—stealing

- *departure from the truth*—deceiving someone

- *deviations from moral rectitude where behaviors are out of synch with inner values or the values of the community*—treating people with disrespect when their respectful treatment is valued.

There is a fourth way to tell right from wrong—the *smell test*, where a behavior feels or smells bad. There is no question as to what is the right choice. We know what to do whether we do it or not.

ETHICAL DILEMMAS

An *ethical dilemma* is a situation where actions to satisfy or act according to one value are in conflict with the desire to satisfy or act according to another. An ethical dilemma is a *right-versus-right* choice. For example:

> Jim and Charlie went on a several-day trek hunting on horseback in a wilderness area. Something spooked Charlie's horse, which lost its footing and fell over, crushing Charlie's leg and side. Charlie was in agony, and Jim quickly saw that there would be no way he could be moved on horseback. It was late afternoon, and the temperature would soon be falling below freezing and Jim knew that Charlie would suffer from hypothermia.
>
> Riding as fast as he could for help, Jim understood it would take at least two days for a rescue attempt. After making Charlie as comfortable as he could, Jim said that he was going for help. Charlie responded, "Bring me my rifle." With the look in Charlie's eyes as he said this, Jim knew what Charlie intended once Jim was gone. What should Jim do?

Jim's dilemma is a right-versus-right choice.

Kidder describes four categories of ethical dilemmas:

- *truth versus loyalty*

- *individual versus community*

- *short term versus long term*

- *justice versus mercy.*

TRUTH VERSUS LOYALTY: This is a choice between telling the truth and acting according to ethical standards or being loyal to another party. For example:

> Betty, a supervisor, receives a call asking for a reference on a former employee, Dick, who was terminated for poor performance. Dick has a family to provide for, and Betty hopes that he will be able to find a new position soon. How open should Betty be in responding to questions about Dick's performance?

Jim's story mentioned above also portrays a truth-versus-loyalty dilemma.

INDIVIDUAL VERSUS COMMUNITY: This dilemma is a choice between acting in self-interest or in the interest of the community. For example:

> John feels exhausted after completing a demanding project at work and just wants to relax over the weekend. His wife and children want him to go with them to the circus in a nearby town for one day. What should John do?

SHORT TERM VERSUS LONG TERM: This dilemma is a choice between doing something of benefit in the short term or deferring action to benefit something in the long term. For example:

> Sally, a single mother, wonders how much to spend on her family's current standard of living versus what she should save for her children's education.

JUSTICE VERSUS MERCY: This dilemma is a choice between administering justice or extending mercy. For example:

Bobby misbehaves on his birthday. Should his mother inflict a lesser punishment than she would normally for such behavior?

Each of these categories is a right-versus-right choice. Often, ethical dilemmas fit more than one category. However, usually one predominates.

RESOLVING ETHICAL DILEMMAS

Rushworth Kidder describes three principles for resolving ethical dilemmas:

- **Ends-based thinking**—Do what is the "greatest good for the greatest number." This principle is called ends-based because it relies upon the consequences or results of an action.

- **Rule-based thinking**—Follow our highest sense of principle or rule. This principle calls upon us to act according to the highest rule of law or moral standard that we would want everyone to act upon in similar circumstances.

- **Care-based thinking**—Do what you would want others to do for you. This principle requires us to empathize with those who would be impacted by our actions and asks us how we would want to be treated if we were in their shoes. This is the "Golden Rule."

Depending upon the ethical dilemma, one or more of these principles may apply. Consider two of the prior dilemma stories.

- *Jim deciding whether to give Charlie's rifle to him*—In this story, all three principles apply. Ends-based thinking is applicable because the result of aiding a friend could be construed as "providing the greatest good to the greatest number," in this case Charlie.

Rule-based thinking, because of the maxim "Thou shall not kill," and its corollary that one should not help someone to do so is perhaps the most relevant. Care-based thinking is also appropriate in that Jim could consider how he would like to be treated if his and Charlie's roles were reversed.

● *John deciding whether to take his family to the circus*—Ends-based thinking appears to be the most appropriate resolution principle in this situation. John can consider the greatest good for the greatest number. He can also consider care-based thinking by asking how he might want to be treated in a similar situation.

It is important to remember that there are no right answers.

In my experience at American Woodmark, some of the most difficult ethical dilemmas I faced were situations where individuals who had long contributed to the organization were no longer able to meet changing job requirements and increased standards of performance. The dilemmas were a combination of "truth versus loyalty" and "the individual versus the community." In many cases, we looked for alternative positions a person could fill, or we waited for them to retire or elect early retirement. In others, we separated them from the company. None of these decisions were easy.

IMPLICATIONS FOR LEADERS

Kidder offers a seven-point checklist that is an effective guide for leaders to resolve ethical dilemmas.

1. **Recognize that there is an ethical dilemma—** Make sure that it is not a right-versus-wrong choice.

2. **Gather the facts**—Establish all of the relevant data necessary to make an informed decision.

3. **Test for the four right-versus-right categories of ethical dilemmas**—Doing so will help frame alternative choices.

4. **Apply the three resolution principles**—Determine which resolution principles are most appropriate and evaluate your alternatives relative to each.

5. **Explore unique or compromise solutions**—Sometimes there is an opportunity for a solution that eliminates or mitigates the dilemma.

6. **Talk to an advisor**—Someone not directly involved in the dilemma can offer help to clarify the relevant issues, assist in seeking unique solutions and help frame alternative choices.

7. **Make a decision**—Once the previous points are completed, all the necessary information is available to make a decision to resolve the dilemma.

This checklist will increase the likelihood that leaders will resolve ethical dilemmas to the best of their abilities and in accordance with their values.

SUMMARY

When we have a right-versus-wrong choice, we know what to do whether or not we do it. There are four categories of ethical dilemmas: "truth versus loyalty," "individual versus community," "short term versus long term" and "justice versus mercy." There are three principles to help resolve ethical dilemmas: ends-based, rule-based and care-based thinking. Using the seven-point checklist increases the likelihood that leaders will resolve ethical dilemmas to the best of their abilities and in accordance with their own values and those of the organization. This tool supports the creation of exceptional organizations and helps to assure that leaders live up to the ethical standards to which they aspire.

FUTURE STUDY

- Think of ethical dilemmas you have faced in the past. Describe the dilemmas and how you resolved them. Ask yourself whether the framework presented in this lesson would have been of use to you in this effort.

- The next time you face an ethical dilemma, use the checklist to assist you in resolving it.

RELATED CHAPTERS

- Essay: Talk is Cheap: 103

- Lesson: Values: 141

SECTION
4

SECTION 4

AN INTERVIEW

This section presents an interview of John P. Howe, III, M.D., President of Project HOPE, an enterprise which has utilized concepts included in this book to assist it in its efforts to create an exceptional organization. It shows the commitment needed for leaders to remain resolute in staying true to their visions while at the same time being adaptable as necessary to get around the inevitable roadblocks and setbacks that come along the way.

Project HOPE, the People—to—People Foundation, was founded by Dr. William Walsh in 1958 with the mission of bringing medical care to people around the globe. Upon its founding, Project HOPE employed the hospital ship HOPE with a cadre of health-care volunteers to carry out its mission. Today, Project HOPE continues its mission of humanitarian aid, operating in 36 countries worldwide and providing over $150 million of goods and services annually.

36

AN INTERVIEW WITH JOHN P. HOWE, III, M.D.

Bill Brandt: John, you decided to use many of the principles and techniques described in this book to support an organizational change initiative for Project HOPE. How did this decision come about?

John Howe: Project HOPE was fortunate in having the leadership of one family—the Walsh family—for many years. I felt honored to join HOPE, in 2001, to continue the traditions of its founder, Dr. William B. Walsh. With my arrival came a shared expectation that we would build upon its current operations, strategy and culture. In 2002, we used a management consulting firm to help us review and reshape our program activities. This effort served us well until 2008, when we agreed that we had the leadership in place to strengthen our culture in ways that would lead to even greater accomplishment.

Bill Brandt: What do you mean by a culture of greater accomplishment?

John Howe: It was a time of high expectations within and without the organization. We were eager to use our current resources—people, time and money—to expand our work through focus and growth in the areas of health education and humanitarian aid. To do so, it would be important for us to come together to achieve a new level of performance throughout the organization made possible by a shared commitment to renewed pace and productivity.

Bill Brandt: What prompted you to use the methodology described in this book?

John Howe: You had recently joined the Project HOPE Board and had brought your experience in leadership training to the organization. We shared our aspirations for HOPE with you. You then described the challenges and opportunities of cultural change. It became very clear that we had an opportunity with your method to realize our goal of greater accomplishment.

Bill Brandt: Before you committed to this direction, you talked with Kent Guichard, the current CEO of America Woodmark, who lived through American Woodmark's journey. Was that a useful dialogue?

John Howe: Yes, absolutely. Here was a real-life, significant business leader looking at you in the eye and saying, "Well John, are you going to do it?" And, so you're sitting there saying: "Oh my gracious, what am I getting myself into?" The interaction was a useful one because it underscored the point that being successful requires the commitment of the leader, and this was a real, not a theoretical, thought. He was making the point—and stirring up a little bit of emotion in me—that this is not for the faint-hearted, but also that, if achieved, would be of great value.

Bill Brandt: You have now been engaged in this initiative for over four years. Have you created everything you wanted to create?

John Howe: The answer is "yes" for the first four years. The effort has had great impact throughout the organization. Our goal was to strengthen our culture in ways that would lead to even greater accomplishment. We have witnessed this throughout the organization. This has been possible by raising the level of leadership—not with a "capital L" but with a "small l" in ways that skills and talents have grown across time zones and continents. We now have a common language of leadership as alumni of this method. With this has come a certain camaraderie and bonding. It has enabled us to do work in ways that we didn't before—with common language, processes and expectations. That said, four years is not the end for us. Our strengthening of the culture continues, as we pursue even greater mastery of this method.

Bill Brandt: How did this transition come about?

John Howe: Our senior leadership went off-site for a three-and-a-half day retreat to begin this leadership training, engaging in the fundamentals of the curriculum. Spending twelve to fifteen hours together each day, we experienced a number of "aha" moments, as we learned a new language and new processes.

Bill Brandt: What would be an example of an "aha" moment?

John Howe: We worked during the day and throughout the evenings as well. For example, on one night, we reviewed the history of HOPE from its beginnings to its legacy; on another, we engaged in dialogue. What I remember most about these sessions was that they were not typical brisk-paced conversations. They were reflective—deliberately filled with periods of silence that gave people time to think before speaking or listening. These sessions were considered to be among the most meaningful parts of the training.

Bill Brandt: What would be another meaningful part?

John Howe: A good example is our senior leadership team meetings. Prior to this course, our experiences were quite variable. People would look at some meetings as being exhilarating but others as uncomfortable and unproductive. We now come to the table with a common set of expectations about how these meetings will flow. We understand the rhythm of the meetings and their expected results, and we feel a sense of a connection to the deliberations. So, it's much more than a checklist of six or seven things to do. It's an opportunity to be much more creative.

Bill Brandt: How easy was it to apply your learning?

John Howe: It was a challenge at the outset. As with learning any new language, it is not something one masters just by taking a course. Facility with a new language is gained by everyday use—and it has been the case with this method as well. In my office, for example, I had the Meeting Management format framed on my wall and right below it that of the 7-Step Process. I regularly referred to them in the early days.

Bill Brandt: What about other people in the organization?

John Howe: The senior leadership retreat was just the beginning. Using the metaphor of a pebble landing in a pond, learning expanded over time in widening rings of involvement throughout the organization. Our goal was to involve our leadership, level by level, starting with our Regional Directors on five continents. We have now conducted five retreats, twenty people at a time, over the past four years.

You led and taught our first retreat. Other members of our senior leadership and I have led about 75 percent of the sessions in subsequent retreats. In addition, we have trained a number of master trainers who teach individual sessions at lower levels in the organization. One of our master trainers is the Director of Internal Audit. Wherever he audits overseas, he teaches core sessions. In addition to those who have attended retreats, over two hundred additional staff have received training at other sessions.

Bill Brandt: You talked about creating a common language for HOPE. Is this feasible when you have people operating in thirty-six different countries?

John Howe: For us, it has been feasible. Most of our nearly five-hundred staff, even those in distant countries, speak

English albeit with different levels of fluency. We have addressed these differences by adjusting the pace of the presentations in keeping with the learner's ability to acquire and retain the new language.

Bill Brandt: What are HOPE's values, and do you see them changing as a result of the culture you are trying to create?

John Howe: Our success in strengthening our culture is related, and directly so, to our values. Three of the four— "respect," "integrity," and "excellence"—are familiar to most organizations. But one is different: "compassion." The word "compassion" goes to the heart of Project HOPE's mission. There's a compassion that is shared with the beneficiary— the mother or child that benefits from our programs. There's also a compassion that's shared with those who are delivering these initiatives—and in some cases rather difficult environments. Similar to your experience at American Woodmark, our cultural change effort is not so much an attempt to change our values but rather an endeavor to live up to them.

Bill Brandt: Did you have any roadblocks along the way?

John Howe: One challenge was that many of us had participated in management programs in the past, and we wanted to avoid the response: "Been there, done that." Another challenge was to ensure that this training would become an everyday part of HOPE. We wanted to avoid the response, "This too shall pass."

Bill Brandt: Anything else?

John Howe: Another challenge was the economic crisis in the United States which occurred early in this four-year period. With over ninety percent of our funding from the private sector, we were not immune to the financial situations of our individual, foundation and corporation donors. It was a perfect storm! We experienced reduced donations, a substantial operating deficit, significantly lower valuations on investment reserves and increased pension liability costs. Since no one could predict the depth or duration of this crisis, we needed a plan to carry us safely through it.

Bill Brandt: How did you create this plan?

John Howe: It was not an easy task. Beginning in October 2008, our senior leadership team along with you met one-half day per week for eight weeks with much additional work done between meetings. We applied the lessons learned in our training sessions in the creation of this plan.

Bill Brandt: What was your desired result?

John Howe: First, we agreed that—after anticipating a significant deficit in fiscal 2009—our financial position should result in a breakeven in 2010 and positive net operating income in 2011. Second, we wanted to protect and enhance our ability to achieve our mission.

Bill Brandt: What was your plan to accomplish this?

John Howe: Once we had this objective, we took a hard look into all aspects of the organization. We needed a clear sense of our current reality. This effort took by far the majority of our planning time. We needed to drastically reduce expenses, but we also needed to invest in critical programs such as electronic fundraising, branding and new business development. We had to make some very difficult choices. We reduced our headquarters staff, while maintaining levels for staff in publishing and in the field overseas. There were no compensation increases for headquarters staff, and our senior leadership took voluntarily compensation reductions. In addition, there were a number of unpaid furlough days for headquarters staff including senior leadership. We replaced our defined benefit plan with a defined contribution plan. However, to continue investing in our people, we maintained our leadership training at all levels of the organization.

Bill Brandt: How did you progress with this plan?

John Howe: We exceeded our plan for 2010, and we achieved our goals for 2011. We have used our resources—people, time and money—wisely and with good result.

Bill Brandt: How do you see your role in leading the organization through this transition?

John Howe: This is not a fad. This is not a here today, gone tomorrow program. This is something that has great value and needs to be woven into the fabric of an organization, and to that end, it won't happen without the tone at the top, without the involvement of the leader. The long-term success is directly related to setting the stage—creating the vision, establishing a design to get there, being very much a part of leading the retreats, teaching modules as part of the training and very importantly, ensuring that the discipline with a "small d" is in fact implemented. This is what I attempted to do.

Bill Brandt: Has everyone been able to make the transition to the new culture you are trying to create?

John Howe: Happily, the predominant response of our people has been very positive. One of the great benefits of the past four years is that we have seen the vast majority of our existing leadership absolutely step up during this difficult time. But like any other program, it would be folly to think that everyone can go forward in lock step. In fact, a very small percentage of our leaders were not able to make the transition. For those who can, however, we recognize that each of us is on his or her own journey, and some participate in their journeys at different paces. We have to make sure that we have patience to provide encouragement. In the end, what we're creating is a culture of accomplishment and that will be the bar that everybody has to leap over. But at this point in time, I've been buoyed by the fact that the overall response has been very positive.

Bill Brandt: Have you experienced a personal transformation in either how you think or act as a leader?

John Howe: The answer is "Yes," and it's seen in every meeting that I lead. I think that if you could contrast my leadership today to three or four years ago, it's different. It's different in the sense that it is much more participatory, more involved.

Bill Brandt: You indicated that you wanted to create a "culture of accomplishment" at HOPE. Has your own leadership style changed as a result of this pursuit?

John Howe: As we have strengthened the culture of HOPE in ways that have led to even greater accomplishment, I have been both a participant and a beneficiary. I have been given the opportunity to learn a new training method—and to use it. I accomplish more at work each day because of its lessons.

Bill Brandt: Have these new behaviors been easy for you to embrace?

John Howe: Again, as with any new language, the early days were often challenging. While I was personally learning new ways of doing work, I was professionally leading others to do the same. It often required the best of "multi-tasking."

Bill Brandt: More than one member of your senior staff has commented to me that they have seen very positive changes in your leadership style. Will you be making additional changes?

John Howe: Yes, for sure. For example, we recently recruited an Executive Vice President who will have operating oversight of 80 percent of the organization. This will require a different—less operations and more policy—type of leadership from me.

Bill Brandt: What is the next step for Project HOPE?

John Howe: The content of this training is not unlike great literature. To fully benefit from it, it must be experienced—

and experienced again. Using the pebble metaphor, we will widen the involvement of our staff including those outside the U.S. We will increase our cadre of master trainers. And, as well, we will implement, in real-life situations around the world, what we learned from our earlier training sessions.

Bill Brandt: You outlined a plan to take the organization through 2011. What are your plans now?

John Howe: When it was clear that our financial plan for 2011 was having a positive effect, we looked beyond it to create what we describe as our "Vision 2015" —what we want to look like in that year? What we're doing is building on the base that was created by our 2011 plan. To use the terminology included in our training, by 2015 we want to be "viable," "sustainable" and "valued," and we have defined what HOPE needs to accomplish to be there.

Bill Brandt: I have one last question for you. If someone were to call you asking your advice on whether or not to take this journey, how would you respond?

John Howe: I'd start by asking a question, "What is it that you want to do?" I would then listen, and depending upon what they said, I would give different advice. If they were simply looking for some form of executive training, then there may be alternative solutions. But if there is a leader that truly aspires to transform his or her organization, then I would describe the HOPE experience—where we created a different culture, a different use of time and different relationships among all of the various parties. What I would do is not unlike what Kent Guichard did with me. I would say on the one hand that this is not for the faint of heart but on the other that it can be unleashing and transforming.

Bill Brandt: Thank you.

MY REFLECTIONS
ABOUT THIS INTERVIEW

The three-and-one-half day leadership retreats mentioned in the interview included all of the lessons in this book with the exception of the lesson, "Vision-Driven Organizations." A particular focus of these retreats was skill-building in the use of the 7-Step Process for both individual and group applications. In the mid-afternoon, participants were divided into three teams to complete projects that reinforced what they learned from the lessons. The topic for the first evening was the dialogue, "Why I came to Project HOPE," the second was a sharing of the early history and legacy of the institution and the third was a question-and-answer session with Dr. Howe and members of his senior leadership team. The agenda for a typical retreat is included in the Appendix at the end of this chapter.

The purpose of the eight half-day strategy sessions referenced by Dr. Howe was to generate a plan that would enable Project HOPE to not only survive the economic crisis that began in 2008, but also to become a viable, sustainable and valued enterprise thereafter. I facilitated these sessions using principles from the lessons, "The 7-Step Process," "Vision-Driven Organizations" and "Mental Models." The planning took as long as it did because of the complexity of Project HOPE's business model. Approximately ten percent of our time was spent creating a vision, seventy-five percent upon understanding current reality and fifteen percent on developing action steps.

I believe that the principles and methodologies employed by Project HOPE are applicable to any type of organization that needs to generate a positive cash flow to support its existence. As a consultant, I have applied these principles to a range of for-profit and non-profit institutions, although Project HOPE is the first organization—other than American Woodmark—

where I have assisted in the creation of a broad-based cultural change effort. From my perspective, the leap of faith with Project HOPE was the degree to which these principles would be accepted across cultures. My belief going into this project was that they would be, but the proof was in the pudding—we needed to verify that this was the case. It's been very gratifying to me to sit beside someone at dinner from Mexico, China or India who affirms that the material makes sense and fits culturally. That has been my experience in talking with people across a full range of countries in which Project HOPE operates.

As for-profit and non-profit enterprises become exceptional, the differences between them become fewer and fewer while the disparity between them and more typical organizations—whether they be for-profit or non-profit—becomes greater and greater. Project HOPE's experience is an excellent example. Within the typical for-profit organization there is often a focus upon *profits* with work organized around this objective. Frequently, such entities have effective performance appraisal systems and a strong sense of accountability to keep them on track. On the other hand, the typical non-profit organization, such as Project HOPE prior to its transition, often organizes its work around its *mission* with the work of the organization kept on track based upon its members' sense of compassion for its beneficiaries. Exceptional organizations, whether for-profit and non-profit, have both a heightened sense of mission and a recognition of the need to generate a positive cash flow. They operate with accountability *and* inspiration and compassion. I think it is very informative that Dr. Howe described wanting to create a "culture of accomplishment" at Project HOPE. He was not saying that he wanted to create a sense of compassion, because Project HOPE had this belief already deeply imbedded into its culture.

It is important to remember that tools and techniques included in this book as adopted by Project HOPE do not have any intrinsic value but are simply a means to an end. I believe that in the future, Project HOPE will develop its own principles and methodologies and that some of these will build upon or replace what is presented in this book.

APPENDIX: LEADERSHIP RETREAT

Each retreat consisted of approximately 20 participants from around the world who held a range of responsibilities at various levels within the organizational hierarchy. As preparation for the retreat participants read essays related most directly to the lessons and watched two movies, *Lorenzo's Oil* and *Twelve Angry Men*. The retreat lasted three and one-half days as shown in Exhibits 36.1 to 36.4

EXHIBIT 36.1 Leadership Retreat: Day 1		
TIME	**TOPIC**	**PRESENTER**
9:00 A.M.	Icebreaker (1)	VP, Human Resources
9:20	Welcome	CEO
9:30	Course Introduction	VP, Human Resources
9:40	Meeting Management (2)	SVP, Programs
10:00	Break	
10:10	7-Step Process	SVP, Programs
10:50	Break	
11:00	Individuals & Organizations in Conflict (3)	Facilitator (4)
11:30	The Exceptional Organization	CEO
12:00 P.M.	Lunch	
1:00	Working in Teams	Director, Internal Audit
1:50	Break	
2:00	Personal Action Plan Exercise	VP, Human Resources
2:50	Team Assignment: Prepare quiz (5)	Facilitator
4:00	Break	
6:00	Dinner	
7:00	Understanding Discourse	Facilitator
7:15	Dialogue: "Why I came to Project HOPE"	Facilitator
8:00	Finish	

1. Each participant met with another participant for five minutes, after which each introduced the other to the full group.

2. All presentations were conducted using PowerPoint™ slides that highlighted the key points of each lesson.

3. This lesson was based upon the essay, "Survival of the Fittest."

4. William F. Brandt, Jr. was the facilitator for the retreat.

5. The group was randomly subdivided into three teams. Each team prepared quiz questions based upon the course material presented that day.

EXHIBIT 36.2   Leadership Retreat: Day 2

TIME	TOPIC	PRESENTER
9:00 A.M.	Check-in & Quiz (1)	Facilitator
9:15	Mental Models (2)	CFO
10:15	Break	
10:30	Personal Action Plan Review	VP, Human Resources
11:30	Lunch	
12:45 P.M.	Values	CEO
1:45	Break	
2:00	Human Motivation	Director, Training
2:35	Break	
3:00	7-Step Process Exercise: "How can our team best learn and apply these teachings over the next six months." Prepare Quiz.	SVP, Programs
4:30	Break	
6:00	Dinner	
7:00	History & traditions of Project HOPE	Long-term Employee
9:30	Finish	

1. Each participant gave a quick comment about what they were thinking or feeling at that moment. The quiz was conducted from the questions created by the teams.

2. The lesson included examples of mental models and a paradigm shift from the movie, *Lorenzo's Oil*.

EXHIBIT 36.3   Leadership Retreat: Day 3

TIME	TOPIC	PRESENTER
8:30 A.M.	Check-in	VP, Human Resources
8:45	Quiz	Facilitator
9:00	Working in Alignment	Director, Internal Audit
9:45	Break	
10:00	Leaders & Followers	VP, Human Resources
10:25	Leadership Styles for Decision Making (1)	VP, Development
10:50	Break	
11:00	Culture	Facilitator
11:15	Cultural Change	Facilitator
12:00 P.M.	Lunch	SVP, Programs
1:00	7-Step Process Exercise: Project HOPE topic	VP, Human Resources
1:45	Team Exercise: "Tying it all together" (2)	Facilitator
3:00	Break	
6:00	Dinner	
7:00	Stories, Dialogue, Questions	CEO and Senior Leadership
8:30	Finish	

1. The movie, *12 Angry Men* was used to highlight examples of leadership styles for decision making.

2. Using art supplies, one team created a mobile, the second a wall presentation and the third a structure rising from the floor. Each design highlighted various aspects of the course learning.

EXHIBIT 36.4   Leadership Retreat: Day 4

TIME	TOPIC	PRESENTER
8:30 A.M.	Check-in	Facilitator
8:45	7-Step Process Exercise: Project HOPE topic	VP, Human Resources
9:30	Break	
9:40	Ethical Dilemmas	VP, Human Resources
10:40	Break	
10:50	Tying it all together and dialogue (1), (2)	Facilitator
12:00 P.M.	Certification, Closing (3)	CEO
12:15	Lunch	
1:00	Depart	

1. The facilitator showed how the lessons combine together to help form an exceptional organization.

2. In the dialogue session participants were asked to reflect upon their experiences with the retreat.

3. All participants received plaques for their participation.

SECTION
5

SECTION 5

IMPLEMENTATION

The essay and lesson sections of this book provide a picture of exceptional organizations—the results achieved, the key elements that drive their behavior and the principles and methodologies that support them. This section describes how to take action to make your vision of an exceptional organization a reality for your enterprise. It includes three chapters.

The first chapter, "Creating and Implementing Your Plan," describes how to develop a "Plan of Action" to guide your actions in this endeavor and offers hints and suggestions that will facilitate this journey. The second, "Using the Materials in this Book," describes the book's website—which offers PowerPoint™ slides of the lessons and versions of the case study, essays, lessons and the interview. Finally, the "Conclusion" shares my closing perspective.

CREATING AND IMPLEMENTING YOUR PLAN

There are two ways to implement the concepts presented in this book. First, you can apply its principles and processes to specific situations as appropriate. For example, if your organization is seeking a new strategy, you can utilize the lesson "Vision-Driven Organizations" to assist you without regard to any other materials presented herein. The subject index at the end of Chapter 2 will help you to match your desired results with the essays and lessons that might best help you in creating those results.

PLAN OF ACTION

A second use of this book is to assist you in creating an exceptional organization by undertaking a broad-based, enterprise-wide initiative. A Plan of Action, as diagramed in Exhibit 37.1, is a guide for such an initiative.

The steps for this plan are as follows.

PLAN OF ACTION

1. *Choose to Implement?* Ask yourself, "Do I want to create an enterprise exhibiting characteristics of an exceptional organization consistent with those stated in this book?" If "yes," then continue.

2. *Have Prerequisites?* As referenced in the essay, "To Be Exceptional," ask yourself:

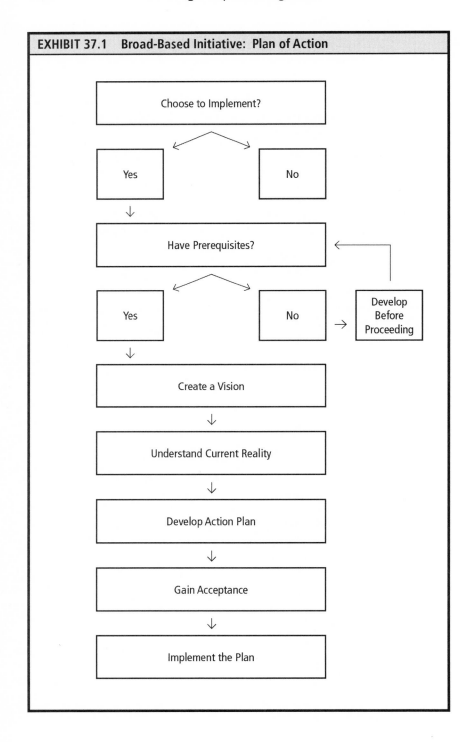

EXHIBIT 37.1   Broad-Based Initiative: Plan of Action

- "Do I have the sense of purpose, values and existing or learnable skills necessary to lead this endeavor?"

- "Does our organization have sufficient resources to sustain us until we create an exceptional organization?"

- "Will our owners or those higher in authority support us as we pursue this transition?"

If you answer "yes" to all three questions, then continue. If you answer "no" to any of them, then take action to resolve the deficiency prior to undertaking an organizational-change effort.

3. *Create a Vision:* Either on your own or with other key stakeholders, create a vision of your organization as being exceptional. This vision should support your organization's purpose and values. You can start by defining what *viable, sustainable* and *valued* means for your institution and then continue with the *key elements* in the same manner. Add any other factors appropriate for your vision not already addressed. The "Introduction" and the lessons "The 7-Step Process" and "Understanding Discourse" can serve as guides for this step and those that follow.

4. *Understand Current Reality:* Describe your organization's current reality relative to the achievement of your vision. Exhibit 37.2 shows a format that can be used as a starting point.

    From this starting point, you can break down more specific aspects of each factor. For example, under the "Vision-Driven" part of your vision, you may note that your people's actions are not in alignment with your organization's purpose.

EXHIBIT 37.2   Current Reality Relative to the Organization's Vision

DESIRED RESULTS	ADEQUATE	INADEQUATE
Viable	❏	❏
Sustainable	❏	❏
Valued	❏	❏

ORGANIZING PRINCIPLES	ADEQUATE	INADEQUATE
Inspiration	❏	❏
Vision-Driven	❏	❏
Value-Based	❏	❏
Right Person/Right Job	❏	❏

5. *Develop Action Steps:* Establish action steps to resolve the discrepancy between your vision and your current reality. For your initial iteration, only the most critical themes need be considered. While some action steps will likely include education and training based upon the principles and methodologies in this book, the majority will be more specific to your organization. You will need to create a hierarchy of action steps as described in the lesson, "Working in Alignment."

6. *Gain Acceptance:* Where possible, create a shared sense of the vision, current reality and action steps from key stakeholders including senior staff, those having authority over the organization and others necessary for a successful implementation. Depending upon the size and complexity of the organization, this process may take a number

of sessions for completion. It is important to realize, however, that the goal is not one of making decisions by consensus. Organization leaders should *consult*—as defined in the lesson, "Leadership Styles for Decision Making"—with their staffs but retain final decision-making authority, for ultimately it is their responsibility for setting the direction of their organizations. It is the staff members' responsibility to accept this direction, even if it is not their preference.

7. *Implement the Plan:* Complete the action steps that will take the organization from its current reality to its vision. Measure the effectiveness of these actions and modify them as necessary until you achieve your desired result. With the scope of such an undertaking, it is likely that there will be significant misdirection, false starts and organizational resistance. The leadership challenge is to stay the course, making adjustments as necessary but not losing sight of the overall objective.

HINTS FOR CREATING AND IMPLEMENTING THE PLAN

Here are some suggestions:

1. *Commitment:* As a leader, you must fully commit to the organizational change. This does not mean that you have all the answers as to how this change will come about, but rather the expectation that you will persevere until you do. As described in the lesson, "Cultural Change," the organization is a stable system, which by definition acts to maintain its existing status, rejecting any attempts to change it. Therefore, it will be imperative that you *hold the vision* even though there will

likely be tremendous pressure for you to abandon or modify it.

2. *The Leader's Behavior:* As a leader, your current behavior is part of the organization's existing culture. To help change the culture, it is critical that you first model any new behaviors that you expect others in your organization to adopt.

3. *The Magnitude of the Task:* The challenges facing an organizational change effort will vary by many factors. All other things being equal, the greater the organization's size, complexity, geographic dispersion, competitive pressures and disparity between its vision and current reality, the greater the task. For some organizations, meaningful results may only take weeks with limited effort, while for others they may require many years with substantial commitments of resources.

4. *No Formula:* Beyond the framework included in the Plan of Action, there is no formula for how best to proceed. Each organization will have a different vision and a different current reality, so the actions taken and the sequence in which they are taken will be unique to each. For example, if one enterprise has a dysfunctional business strategy, while another one's is quite adequate, the appropriate actions will necessarily vary significantly.

5. *Time Frames:* Be realistic in setting time frames for achieving your goals. Anticipate and allow for potential resistance to action steps. Also, realize that at times unanticipated events will likely take precedence over your organizational-change initiative.

6. *Create Stepping Stones Toward Your Vision:* In some situations, the magnitude of your vision may

appear overwhelming. If this is the case, consider breaking down your overall vision into a series of goals that will be more readily achievable. A key responsibility of the leader is to effectively manage the degree of tension between the vision and the current reality. Too little tension results in too little movement. Too much tension may result—like the snapping of a rubber band—in disbelief, resignation and again, little movement. The objective is to maintain a "stretch" in perceived effort by successively creating challenging but achievable goals. For example, your vision may be to completely replace your existing product line within five years. You may wish to create separate goals for what you need to accomplish each year.

7. *Cultural Change:* Merely describing a culture—such as articulating new values, beliefs and traditions—in and of itself will not result in any significant change in behavior. Behaviors change when they are fostered and reinforced by new tools and processes that support elements of the desired culture. Therefore, to avoid any perceived sense of hypocrisy, it is important that leaders, at the start of a cultural-change effort, describe "acting in accordance with the new culture" as a vision to be aspired to rather than as a reality already in place.

8. *Honor the Past:* Build the culture upon the positive aspects of the existing culture. Honor the past rather than be dismissive of it. Realize that each generation of an organization stands upon the shoulders of the one that preceded it. Being dismissive of the past takes away the organization's sense of roots and tradition and discredits

the contributions of those still in the organization who had worked in those times.

9. *Changing in Good Times:* It is more difficult to change an organization when times are good than when they are bad. In good times, people embrace the status quo, but in bad times they fear it. The challenge when things are going well is to make people aware that if the organization does not change, the good times may soon be over. This will not be easy to sell. You may need to settle for "grudging compliance," as described in the lesson, "Leaders and Followers."

10. *Use of a Consultant:* It may be advantageous to have a consultant to facilitate this process. It is critical, however, that the change effort be identified as being led by senior leadership rather than as being delegated to a consultant. This identification will happen only if senior leadership is significantly involved in implementing this plan by modeling behaviors and teaching others to do the same.

11. *Senior Leadership Role in Training:* As soon as feasible, leaders and their senior managers should conduct most if not all of the training for key personnel. This task should not be delegated. At lower levels in the organization, the training should be conducted by those higher in authority but not necessarily the senior leadership team. Consider using level-to-level training for those aspects of the change effort that require across-the-board adoption of new beliefs and the learning of new tools. With this approach, members at the highest level in the organization first learn and apply the new principles and skills and then successively train those at the next lower level until

everyone at each level of the hierarchy has adopted them.

12. *What Materials to Use and When to Use Them:*
Depending upon the organization's needs, some of
the materials in this book may be of benefit while
others may not. For example, for multi-level enterprises the lesson "Cultural Change" may be
appropriate for mid-level management and above
but not for those at lower levels. The next chapter, "Using the Materials in this Book's Website,"
shows leaders how they can personalize their presentations.

13. *Quick Results:* While there is no formula for se-
quencing the use of the material in this book, the
lessons, "Meeting Management" and "The 7-Step
Process," are both tools which have the potential
of generating effective results quickly. They will
likely enhance work performance, begin the formation of a collective language across the organization and generate momentum toward creating
a new culture.

14. *Offsite Retreats:* A particularly effective way to
facilitate cultural change, especially for larger organizations, is a four-to-five day offsite retreat led
by senior management. Such a retreat could provide for up to twenty-five people in a session with
those attending coming from various management
levels, functional areas and geographic regions. In
addition to the specific training, time can be spent
in team-building exercises, story-telling, dialogue
and free time with other participants. Attendees
are typically impacted as much or more by these
activities as by the material presented. Furthermore, they are likely to leave such a session with

a much greater connection and commitment to the organization and a greater sense of self.

15. *Relieving Barriers to Change:* Anticipate resistance to any change initiative. As described in the lesson, "Cultural Change," focus as much or more effort on relieving barriers to change as you do to promoting benefits. Key to this endeavor will be to help people to change their mental models, many of which will be held with deep emotional commitment.

16. *People's Ability to Change:* The vast majority of the people will make the conversion to the new culture. However, some will be unable to make the transition because they either cannot perform new job responsibilities or are unwilling to act according to its values. The higher the level of individuals in the organization, the more critical will it be that they be servant leaders who embrace the enterprise's mission, values and beliefs. If they do not, these individuals must leave the enterprise either through their own volition or that of the organization.

17. *Achieving Critical Mass:* At some point, you will reach a critical mass where the impetus to change to a new culture will become greater than the impetus to maintain the status quo. Reaching this point will be arduous and time consuming. Once reached, however, progress will be made more quickly and with less effort.

SUMMARY

Using the Plan of Action and the hints for creating and implementing a plan as a guide, you will significantly increase the likelihood that you will create the organization you desire and do so as effectively and efficiently as reasonable. To repeat again, never lose sight of your vision, but be flexible in your approach to getting there. Modify your actions as appropriate. A successful journey will be more than worth the effort.

38

USING MATERIALS FROM THIS BOOK'S WEBSITE

This book's website offers the opportunity to customize materials for specific audiences. You can download electronic files of the American Woodmark case study, the interview with Dr. Howe, the implementation plan and each of the essays and lessons. In addition, you can download PowerPoint™ slides of each lesson for use in making group presentations. Each selection is self-contained, meaning that it has been modified so that it does not reference any other parts of the book. By so doing, only the relevant material need be considered, and it can be used in any sequence desired.

There is no fee for your sharing material with up to five users. A user is defined as any individual who receives any of the materials in printed form or who attends a lesson presentation. For additional users, there is a per-user fee, which you can pay by credit card at the website.

This book's website is: CompassCEO.com.

39

CONCLUSION

The traditional view of economic reality holds that the pursuit of "self-interest" benefits not only individuals but also society. While we acknowledge the past successes of this premise, we have become increasingly aware of its limitations. This book postulates a new more powerful paradigm, one that advocates the simultaneous pursuit of both "self-interest" *and* "concern for others." The key to living according to this new paradigm is the creation of exceptional organizations—ones that are *viable*, in that they achieve their purposes and act according to society's highest values; *sustainable*, in that they remain viable over time and *valued*, in that they benefit all stakeholders to a superior degree.

An organization can facilitate its quest to become viable, sustainable and valued by adopting:

- a shared vision of the organization's aspirations
- a shared understanding of its current reality
- appropriate action steps, including an effective business strategy
- common beliefs and values
- highly effective and universally applicable tools and processes
- a common language across the enterprise.

As these attributes are embraced, the organization will likely reach a critical mass after which it will quickly move toward becoming exceptional.

Because every organization that seeks to become exceptional has a different desired result and a different starting point, each will follow its own unique path to get there. By providing various principles and techniques—a *compass*—this book will help you along your way.

As mentioned in the Introduction, this book is intended for those leaders, who in their hearts and minds, are already committed to creating organizations consistent with this new paradigm. For such leaders, my intent is not to overpromise those whose organizations' do not have the necessary prerequisites for success but rather to encourage them to develop these capacities before undertaking such a venture. For those who's entities do have these prerequisites, I encourage them to take this journey. While the challenges are real and there is no guarantee of success, the potential results are extraordinary, and a successful outcome is not only feasible but likely. There is the possibility of many more exceptional organizations in this world. The expansion of such institutions will benefit not just individual organizations and their members but also humankind.

ENDNOTES

CHAPTER 5

[1] Rand, Ayn. *The Virtues of Selfishness*. New York: 1961, x.

CHAPTER 7

[1] Neff, Thomas J. and James M. Citrin. *Lessons from the Top*. New York: Doubleday, 1999.

[2] Manual, Dave. "The Seven Most Crooked CEO's of All Time," *Dave Manuel.com Newsletter*, April 26, 2008.

[3] Collins, Jim. *Good to Great*. New York: Harper Business, 2001, 21.

CHAPTER 12

[1] *Wall Street*. Beverly Hills, California: Twentieth Century Fox Film, 1987.

[2] Smith, Adam. *The Theory of Moral Sentiments,* Edited by D. D. Raphael and A. L. Macfie. Oxford, England: Clarendon Press, 1976.

CHAPTER 15

[1] *American Law Institute's Principles of Corporate Governance*. Egan, Minnesota: West Publishing, 2008, 55.

[2] This observation was made by Robert Fritz as part of a seminar he conducted titled, *Structural Approach to Leadership*. Toronto: June 4-5, 2009.

[3] *American Law Institute's Principles of Corporate Governance,* 414.

CHAPTER 16

[1] Enron Corporation. *Code of Ethics*, Internal Document. Houston: July, 2000, 1.

CHAPTER 20

[1] Collins, Jim. *Good to Great*. New York: Harper Business, 2001, 32.

CHAPTER 21

[1] Frankl, Victor E. *Man's Search for Meaning*. New York: Simon and Schuster, 1984, 16-17.

CHAPTER 23

[1] Kidder, Rushworth M. *How Good People Make Tough Choices: Resolving the Dilemmas of Ethical Living*. New York: HarperCollins Publishers, 2003, 81-82.

CHAPTER 25

[1] Based upon a lesson created by James (Jake) Gosa. *Unpublished Presentation Notes*. 1997.

[2] Senge, Peter M. *The Fifth Discipline*. New York: Doubleday, 1990, 219-220.

CHAPTER 28

[1] Sipress, David. *Cartoon: The New Yorker*. New York: Conde Nast, October, 31 2011, 64.

CHAPTER 30

[1] National Association of Realtors. *Existing Home Prices*. Washington, D.C., 2012. The existing home price index dropped from 221.9 for 2006 to 166.1 for 2011.

[2] Downes, Robert B. *Books That Changed The World*. New York: Penguin Books, 1956, 182.

CHAPTER 32

[1] Katzenbach, Jon R. and Douglas K. Smith. *The Wisdom of Teams*. New York: Harper Collins, 2002, 45.

BIBLIOGRAPHY

Alland Jr., Alexander. *Human Nature: Darwin's View*. New York: Columbia University Press, 1985.

American Law Institute's Principles of Governance. Egan, Minnesota: West Publishing, 2008.

Briggs, John & F. David Peat. *Turbulent Mirror*. New York: Harper & Row, 1990.

Chaleff, Ira. *The Courageous Follower*. San Francisco: Berrett-Koehler Publishers, 1995

Christensen, Clayton M. *The Innovator's Dilemma*. Boston: Harvard Business School Press, 1997.

Collins, Jim. *Good to Great*. New York: Harper Business, 2001.

Darwin, Charles. *The Descent of Man*. Lexington, Kentucky: Pacific Publishing Studio, 2011.

Darwin, Charles. *The Origin of Species*. Edited by J. W. Burrow. London: Penguin Books, 1958.

Downes, Robert B. *Books That Changed The World*. New York: Penguin Books, 1956.

Eisler, Riane. *The Challice and the Blade*. New York: HarperCollins, 1987

Enron Corporation. *Code of Ethics*, Internal Document. Houston: July, 2000.

Frankl, Victor E. *Man's Search for Meaning*. New York: Simon and Schuster, 1984.

Fritz, Robert. *The Path of Least Resistance*. New York: Fawcett Columbine, 1989.

Fritz, Robert. *The Path of Least Resistance for Managers*. San Francisco: Berrett-Koehler Publishers, 1999.

Fritz, Robert. Seminar—*Structural Approach to Leadership*. Toronto: June 4-5, 2009.

Fritz, Robert. *Your Life as Art*. Newfane, Vermont: Newfane Press, 2003.

Gilligan, Carol. *In a Different Voice*. Cambridge, Massachusetts: Harvard University Press, 1993.

Gosa, James (Jake). *Unpublished Presentation Notes*, 1997.

Greenleaf, Robert K. *Servant Leadership*. New York: Paulish Press, 1977.

Guichard, Kent. *Unpublished Documents*, 1994.

Katzenbach, Jon R. and Douglas K. Smith. *The Wisdom of Teams*. New York: Harper Collins, 2002.

Kidder, Rushworth M. *How Good People Make Tough Choices*. New York: Harper Collins, 1995

Kidder, Rushworth M. *Shared Values for a Trouble World*. San Francisco: Josey-Bass Publishers, 1994.

Loye, David. *Darwin's Lost Theory*. Carmel, California: Benjamin Franklin Press, 2010.

Lorenzo's Oil. Universal City, California: Universal Studios, 1992.

Manual, Dave. "The Seven Most Crooked CEO's of All Time," *Dave Manuel.com Newsletter*, April 26, 2008.

McLean, Bethany and Peter Elkind. *The Smartest Guys in the Room*. London: Penguin Books, 2003.

National Association of Realtors. *Existing Home Prices*. July, 2010.

Neff, Thomas J. and James M. Citrin. *Lessons from the Top*. New York: Doubleday, 1999.

O'Brien, William J. *Character and the Corporation*. Unpublished Document

O'Brien, William J. *The Soul of Corporate Leadership; Guidelines for Value-Centered Governance.* Waltham, Massachusetts: Pegasus Communications, 1998.

Rand, Ayn. *The Virtues of Selfishness.* New York: Signet, 1961.

Senge, Peter M. *The Fifth Discipline.* New York: Doubleday, 1990.

Sipress, David. *Cartoon: The New Yorker.* New York: Condé Nast: October, 31 2011.

Stalk, Jr., George. "Time-The Next Source of Competitive Advantage," *Harvard Business Review.* Boston: Harvard Business School Publishing Division, July-August, 1988.

Taleb, Nassim Nicholas. *The Black Swan.* New York: Random House, 2007.

Tannenbaum, Robert and Warren H. Schmidt. "How to Choose a Leadership Pattern," *Harvard Business Review.* Boston: Harvard Business School Publishing Division, March-April 1958.

The Bridge on the River Kwai. Culver City, California: Columbia Pictures, 1957.

Twelve Angry Men. Beverly Hills, California: Metro-Goldwyn-Mayer Studios, 1957

Vandenberg, Roger. *Unpublished Notes*, 2010.

INDEX

ACKNOWLEDGMENTS

This book reflects what I have learned over the course of my career, and therefore there are a multitude of people who helped shape its creation. I appreciate the contributions of all current and prior employees of American Woodmark: especially cofounders Al Graber, Jeff Holcomb and Don Mathias; the leaders who succeeded me as CEO, Jake Gosa and Kent Guichard; and Dave Blount, a member of our senior leadership team. I am indebted to Robert Fritz and Peter Senge, whose concepts are integral to this book and to George Stalk, whose ideas were fundamental to American Woodmark's strategic direction. I am thankful for the advice and counsel of Bill O'Brien and Dr. Lester Tobias, who have been mentors to me. I am also grateful to those who have applied the principles in this book to their respective organizations, and in particular John Howe, III, M.D., President of Project HOPE and John Lamanna, Executive Director of Timber Ridge School.

For the actual development of this book, I am indebted to Charles Dorris, developmental editor; Carolyn Porter, editor and book producer; Alan Gadney, book-marketing advisor; Liz Hamilton, graphic designer and Justin Ruble, copy editor. A very special thank you goes to Todd Robinson, who read every draft of this book and who provided encouragement and invaluable insight along the way.

For reading drafts of the book or for making other contributions, I wish to thank: Brian Allen, Jeffery Arnold, Kate Buford, Douglas Clark, Robert Claytor, Michael Curro, Dr. James Davis, Andrew Ferrari, Dr. Tracy Fitzsimmons, Steven (Spike) Karalekas, Reynold (Pete) Mooney, Dayton Ogden, Hager Patton, Thomas Richards, Vance Tang, Roger Vandenberg, and Miriam Wardak.

I also wish to thank my assistant Kristy Walker who provided me with invaluable support throughout this endeavor. I am very grateful for my daughter Alison and the memory of my daughter Sarah. I wish to express my deep appreciation to my wife Elaine, who has been by my side from the time that American Woodmark was no more than an idea to the completion of this book.

ABOUT THE AUTHOR

 **William F. Brandt Jr.** is a cofounder and former CEO of American Woodmark Corporation, which was formed in 1980 to acquire Boise Cascade Corporation's kitchen cabinet business. American Woodmark is the third largest cabinet manufacturer nationally, serving The Home Depot, Lowe's and major builders. Sales have grown from $35 million to over $600 million. The company went public in 1986.

Brandt has written for numerous publications, and consults in the areas of CEO coaching, leadership development, strategic planning and cultural change. He serves on a number of for-profit and non-profit boards including a university, a health-care system, a hospital, and an international humanitarian aid organization.

Brandt has degrees from Dartmouth College and its Tuck School of Business. He is Executive-in-Residence at the Harry F. Byrd, Jr. School of Business at Shenandoah University, where he is also a member of their Adjunct Faculty. He lives in Winchester, Virginia with his wife Elaine and their golden retriever Daisy.

COMPASS

Additional copies are available
through your favorite bookstore
or from the book's website below.

Reading Materials
and
Presentation Slides

Electronically formated reading materials
and PowerPoint™ presentation slides
based on the book are available
from the website:
www. CompassCEO.com

For inquiries, please E-mail:
ContactUs@CompassCEO.com